Eng. by John Sartain Phil.a

Yrs Very Truly
John M. Lowrie

ADAM AND HIS TIMES

BY
JOHN M. LOWRIE, D. D.
AUTHOR OF "ESTHER AND HER TIMES.
PASTOR OF THE FIRST PRESBYTERIAN CHURCH,
FORT WAYNE, INDIANA.

"No age
Can outgrow truth, or can afford to part
With the tried wisdom of the past, with words
That centuries have sifted, and on which
Ages have set their seal."

BONAR.

PHILADELPHIA:
PRESBYTERIAN BOARD OF PUBLICATION,
No. 821 CHESTNUT STREET.

STEREOTYPED BY WILLIAM W. HARDING, PHILADELPHIA.

PREFACE.

THESE chapters do not pretend to discuss their grave topics with the critical learning that might befit the theological chair. It is indeed important that all Scriptural doctrines should be truthfully and accurately stated; but it is an excellency of the Bible that it reserves no doctrines for a special class of disciples. It is a Revelation, and it invites every man to become a learner. We recognize no such difference between the pupils in a theological school, and the readers of a religious book, or the hearers in a Christian sanctuary, as to allow that the first are to be taught doctrines which they are not in turn to transmit to their hearers. The book is for all; the same substantial teachings each believer needs, that he may become a perfect man in Christ Jesus; the same truths give vigour to piety in any sphere of duty. And if we may grant that the ministry of the gospel, set for the defence and the interpretation of the truth, should have a critical acquaintance with the sacred text, and a wider range of information touching the views of opposers and errorists; even this difference, which regards only the manner and extent of the teachings they receive and not the doctrines themselves, is a difference less plainly marked in our own times than formerly. For now every man is a reader; the press vies with the pulpit in discussing sacred themes; and hundreds of men, all over the land, are ready to receive the judicious discussion of any Scriptural teachings.

The doctrines here treated of belong to every age of the Church, and are traced back to the earliest period of revealed religion; and no intelligent man can judge them unsuitable for the instruction of a Christian people. Yet it is perhaps true that they are less discussed among us, than in the days of our fathers. But may it not be that the stirring activity of our times needs a larger admixture of their thoughtful training in those sterling doctrines, that have never been neglected without enervating the piety of the Church, and never been received without invigorating it?

These pages contain the substance of a course of lectures given to the congregation of which the author is pastor. They are not printed as originally spoken. Many practical thoughts and exhortations have been omitted, and this partly because the manuscript was not used in the pulpit. The reasons which induced their original preparation may justify their wider circulation by means of the press. They are such as these: All Scripture is given by inspiration of God, and is profitable. The people of God have a right to all the teachings of his word; the entire scheme of salvation cannot be presented, nor the symmetry of any parts be preserved, if these things are omitted. The Scriptural method of teaching doctrine is not in the abstract form, but in connection with the events of life and history which call forth the doctrine, and illustrate it, and give it interest. An intelligent people cannot be formed under any ministry that does not take pains to give careful instruction. The more patient thought is demanded of any people, the more fully will they rise to it, provided their interest can be awakened; and finally, the press is the most fitting means of teaching truths which require more mature thought than can be given at a single hearing.

The theology of the book accords, it is believed, with that of the old Calvinistic divines. No effort is made at an unattainable originality upon themes sixty centuries old. There will be found, indeed, no servile copying of any human master; but our respect is profound for the Scriptural writers. Of them we cannot say more, and desire not to say less, than that the longer we study them the deeper is our conviction that "holy men of old spake," not by the promptings of human wisdom, but "as they were moved by the Holy Ghost."

If things are found here that others have said before, let the words of an ancient critic be a sufficient defence. They who are competent to make the charge will respect the authority. "Quum pravum quoddam (ut arbitror) studium circa scriptores artium exstiterit, nihil eisdem verbis, quæ prior aliquis occupasset, finiendi; quæ ambitio procul aberit a me." Quint. Inst. Orat. Lib. II. C. xv. § 37.

CONTENTS

CHAPTER I.

THE RELATION OF THE OLD TESTAMENT TO THE NEW.

PAGE

Christ came not to destroy the law; he fulfils its types, and predictions; and the moral law. Law and gospel harmonize. O. T. Scriptures not superseded: consistent with the New. Christ gave his sanction to the ancient Scriptures: indeed they are more instructive now than ever—Religious experience of ancient believers profitable........ 13

CHAPTER II.

OLD TESTAMENT BIOGRAPHIES.

Past ages live in history and biography. We need faithful delineations. Scriptural descriptions truthful. We get just ideas of the persons—Hard to decide what allowance to make. These are our examples........ 22

CHAPTER III.

THE FIRST MAN.

Life of the first man interesting. His influence ever felt. "The Son of God." A perfect man. "Very good." His knowledge, uprightness, immortality, conscience. Thoughts upon conscience........ 28

CHAPTER IV.

ADAM IN PARADISE.

Eden. A beautiful spot—Like heaven. Liable to fall. A tiller of the ground—Employment a blessing—Not lawless, but in subjection—Self-denial an essential element of earthly piety. Our happiness........ 34

CHAPTER V.

THE GARDEN AND ITS TREES.

PAGE

Many opinions respecting Eden. Its site—Discrepant views—Trees of beauty and food. Vegetable food—Two trees—The tree of knowledge—The tree of life.......... 40

CHAPTER VI.

MARRIAGE AS GIVEN IN EDEN.

First social institution. Ordained of God. Two parties—Eve a helpmeet. Marriage honourable—Unwise restrictions—Permanent—Ruled by love—Divorce—Value shown by tendency to corruption—Evils of our time. An aged couple. A happy land where the Scriptural ordinance is maintained.......... 45

CHAPTER VII.

THE ORIGIN AND PERPETUITY OF THE SABBATH.

Sabbath in Eden—Not a Jewish institution—For man innocent and more needed now. Observed before Moses; predicted after Christ; for man. The change of day argues perpetuity. Only perpetual things retained under the gospel—Paul's meaning.......... 67

CHAPTER VIII.

NATURE, DESIGN, AND DUTIES OF THE SABBATH.

Sacred obligations of the day—Men want a Sunday—A desecrated Sabbath undesirable—Proper use—The original—More needed since the fall—Especially in our age—Steam and labour—The poor—U. S.—Like marriage, a family institution—This secures all the rest—Baxter—Holy time—Important question—France—A type of heaven. Paradise lost and regained...... 76

CHAPTER IX.

THE ORIGIN OF EVIL.

The Labyrinth—How sin? Theories. "God the Author of Sin." "A necessary evil." Incredible and mischievous—The guiding thread—We must acknowledge facts—God sovereign and man free—Permitted: in sovereignty and wisdom.......... 86

CHAPTER X.

THE GREAT TEMPTER.

PAGE
The serpent—Satan—Scriptural teachings of him.................... 94

CHAPTER XI.

MAN'S FIRST SIN.

Some think the first sin insignificant. Serious for many reasons —Threatening and promise—Representative—Adam knew it. Personal duty. This offence serious—The chief of sinners..... 98

CHAPTER XII.

THE TEMPTATION.

Brief sketches—Eve—Tempter's manner—sight of the tree—distrust—gradual—Adam tempted—Good and evil—Unwilling to meet God—Falsehood; self-justification; impenitence......... 106

CHAPTER XIII.

THE GOSPEL ANNOUNCED.

The tempter first judged—The serpent—Satan—The conflict—Germ of the gospel—The Seed is Christ—Traditions. Christ's people—A long struggle and its results............................. 114

CHAPTER XIV.

THE SENTENCE UPON EVE.

Not on Eve alone—Woman more religious than man. Spiritual interests—A blessing to the race—mothers—Crowning virtue.. 124

CHAPTER XV.

LABOUR.

Ground cursed; yet labour needful—Weeds, &c., employment, and toil—Scriptural generalization—Agriculture represents all labour. Toil—Not purely a curse—Honourable industry....... 130

CHAPTER XVI.

DEATH.

Is man mortal by constitution? Various pains and ills: wars: violence: &c... 140

CHAPTER XVII.

THE CURSE UPON THE RACE.

PAGE

Evils upon all men. Universal sinfulness, and connected with Adam—Scripture statements—Dr. Dwight's arguments—Sinful by nature as truly as rational—Entire depravity. Meaning of total depravity—Facts—Philosophy—We must classify facts—Providential as well as Biblical—Explanations not fully satisfactory. The Scriptural solution superior..................... 148

CHAPTER XVIII.

PRELIMINARY STATEMENTS.

True teachings, and man's conceptions of them—Progress of opinion and true science—Astronomy—N. T. truths clearer—Practical benefit and theoretical ignorance—Use of laws not understood. The early and the late where true, consistent—Facts concerning Adam, plain for ages—Adam Representative. 159

CHAPTER XIX.

DEFINITION OF TERMS.

Covenant of works—Federal Head—Imputation—Guilt............ 165

CHAPTER XX.

WHENCE THE AUTHORITY OF A REPRESENTATIVE?

Principles of representation familiar—Adam not merely a father—Representation just, wise, and needful—Ground of Adam's authority—Inquiry respecting choice. Government divine as an ordinance. How far in human hands? A legal representation of those that voted against and not at all—Divine appointment, where it can be ascertained, the best possible basis of authority. The *fact* in Adam's case proves the *right*......... 170

CHAPTER XXI.

THE COVENANT MADE WITH ADAM—REASONABLE ARGUMENTS.

Worthy of God's wisdom—Man under law—A covenant changes—Advantages—Had Adam stood, the gratitude of the race—Difficulties in any view—"Voluntary nature of man." "Evil examples." "Divine constitution." No progress made by such solutions. A covenant less difficulties and superior advantages. 177

CHAPTER XXII.

THE COVENANT MADE WITH ADAM—SCRIPTURAL ARGUMENTS.

Genesis—Parties, terms, penalties of covenant—Circumstances all consistent with this view. God's usual methods—Covenant

PAGE
often spoken of—Noah, Abraham, David, &c. Scriptural references. Hosea, Corinthians, Romans V.—Infants—Adam's *one* offence—Practical influence........................... 187

CHAPTER XXIII.

ADAM, THE FIRST AND THE SECOND.

Early knowledge of redemption—Adam knew Christ truly—Adam and Christ representative—Paul's illustration—Not entirely alike—Both public persons. Proof......................... 196

CHAPTER XXIV.

THE AFFILIATED DOCTRINES.

Principles implied—Representation—Imputation—Sin and righteousness—Analogies and differences—Federal Headship—Objections—Light upon each other.................................... 203

CHAPTER XXV.

THE SECOND ADAM GREATER.

Parallel not complete. The Second greater—Condemnation by law. Salvation by *grace*—Recovery more difficult—One and many—More than restored—Perplexities—Grounds of faith—Precious invitations. Happy they who make this covenant... *208*

CHAPTER XXVI.

ADAM'S FIRST BORN SONS.

First parents repentant. Skins of beasts—Paradise left—First born—Parental love and duty—Disappointment—Differences of character, occupation, worship.................................. 218

CHAPTER XXVII.

THE WORSHIP OF CAIN.

Early worship—Mistake of reason—Man a sinner—Bloody sacrifices — Prophecy — Faith — Revelation and Reason. First errorist—Works of righteousness. Woe to the way of Cain... 225

CHAPTER XXVIII.

THE REJECTION OF CAIN.

Results. Fire from heaven—Rage and impenitence—Long-suffering mercy—Expostulation. Increasing sin. Faith—Murmuring unprofitable—Convictions lead to God or harden..... 231

CHAPTER XXIX.

THE SACRIFICE OF ABEL.

PAGE

Sacrifice — The animals offered: significancy — Ceremonies— Honourable confessions. Sympathy with erring — Abel's offering—Blood of sprinkling.. 237

CHAPTER XXX.

THE DEATH OF ABEL.

Gradual separation of the brothers. Men of mature life. A hundred years of sin—Dreadful deed--Parental grief—First human death—Honour of Abel—Joy in heaven..................... 244

CHAPTER XXXI.

THE CRIMINAL EXPOSED.

Concealment—Conscience—God speaks. Brother's keeper—Falsehood vain—Webster's speech. Circumstantial evidence —Necessary: Satisfactory... 252

CHAPTER XXXII.

CAPITAL PUNISHMENT.

Cain's apprehensions. Arguing against capital punishments—Mosaic laws—Noah and all nations—Public and private deeds—We need every safeguard—The Divine Law—Life insecure..... 260

CHAPTER XXXIII.

THE PUNISHMENT OF CAIN.

Why death remitted to Cain? Disproof of justice—Sovereign privilege — Who would execute the penalty? Why fear? Conscience.. 269

CHAPTER XXXIV.

CALLING UPON THE LORD.

Time softens grief—Seth—Eight generations—Calling upon the Lord. Profanity. Prayer—Public worship—Revivals of religion—Interest and anxiety. Church and world divided. Adam's deep concern.. 276

CHAPTER XXXV.

LONG LIFE.

Longevity—Adam's adult life—Traditions to Jacob—Life shortened. Gen. vi.-xi. Moral reasons—Would we better prepare —One sinner destroyeth much—Time enough. No account of Adam's death. Time and eternity...................................... 284

ADAM AND HIS TIMES.

CHAPTER I.

THE RELATION OF THE OLD TESTAMENT TO THE NEW.

This word divine, which on the desert sands,
  On Judah's sacred hills, on Babel's plains,
Was penned by Moses', David's, Daniel's hands;
  Which precious gospel, righteous law contains,
  And God's great mystery to man explains;
Prophetic, promising the woman's seed,
  Historic, telling of his wondrous birth,
His wondrous words, his death for man's great need,
  Doth by God's Spirit teach the sons of earth,
And chiefly doth reveal a Saviour's work and worth.

THE words of our Lord Jesus Christ, "I am not come to destroy the law, but to fulfil it," are true, in a remarkable degree, of the entire Old Testament writings. He indeed fulfils the shadowy teachings of the ceremonial law. And he also answers many of the remarkable predictions made by the ancient prophets. Still further, in every just sense of the term, he sustains the moral law; which, in the proper use of language, is the *law* of God. Under that law he was voluntarily made, (Gal. iv. 4,) when he assumed our nature as the Mediator between God and man. His entire life was in obedience to that law; his teachings supported the spirit and principles, the precepts and the penalties of that law; his expiatory death was under the sentence of that law; and, different as his gospel is from the law in nature and influence, yet no man ever partakes of the blessings of the gospel of Christ, who does not approve of the law of God as "holy, and wise, and good;" Rom. vii. 12; and who is not cheerfully subject to the guidance of the law. Great as are the differences between law and grace, they harmonize in glorifying the same God, and in demanding a like holiness; and a true believer in the gospel of Christ is a lover, invariably, of the law of God. A teacher who makes the law of perpetual obligation; who vindicates its true teachings from the glosses of error; who honours it in every aspect, and that in the most remarkable and illustrious manner; and who is succeeded by a race of disciples whose purity of doctrine and purity of life combine to promote his cause, may justly claim to support the law of God.

But if this is the direct force of our Lord's words, it is true also that they mean more. The entire Scriptures, as already in the hands of men, are sustained by him, as he fulfils the law. These Old Testament writings are neither so clear nor so full in their teachings of religious truth, as are the writings of the New Testament. When the Son of God is manifest in the flesh, we may look for revelations in advance of any thing before granted to prophets that were merely human. Perhaps some minds might anticipate that the New would supersede the Old: that the servants would be allowed to step entirely aside since their Lord had come. But this would be to overlook the great fact that these servants owed their wisdom and authority to a Divine commission. With this in view, we may rather judge that the teachings of Christ should be in full harmony with all that had gone before. Just as it is with all the truths we learn in our childhood, that they remain true, even when the clearer conceptions of riper years enable us to know the same things better; just as the earlier astronomers learned much of the positions and motions of the heavenly bodies, and the telescope enables us in modern times to learn more of the same things; just as, to say nothing of the errors and misconceptions in both these cases, all the earlier truths are in full harmony with the later truths: so, in the Scriptures of the Old and New Testaments, the revelations of the Holy Spirit are all true, and therefore all consistent with each other. It may be then that the early church did not understand as we do; it may be that the late prophets are superior, and especially so is the Lord of all the prophets. But it would be very strange to find any contradiction between them, or any necessity for repealing the earlier teachings;

since all these teachings are of Divine authority, and the earlier servants were sent by the same Lord. That they were ignorant of things we now know: that they misconceived the meaning, or could not understand the meaning of some things they had: that they predicted the future less for themselves than for us, (1 Peter i. 12,) may all be true, without implying that the teachings of the New Testament are designed to set aside the teachings of the Old.

And it is really found that, taking the Old Testament as a whole, Jesus Christ came not to destroy but to confirm and establish it. The old economy gives place to the new: as we are taught in several passages of Paul, Heb. viii., Gal. iii. But by this is meant—not that the Scriptures of the Old Testament teach us less than before, or are less profitable for rebuke and instruction—only, that the Jewish people no longer stand in the peculiar position assigned to them by the regulations given at Sinai, and in the wilderness. The arrangements made with them were temporary, till the seed should come to whom the promise had been made more than four centuries earlier. Gal. iii. 17, 19. Yet when we make decided and important advantages belong to the Christian dispensation as compared with the Patriarchal and the Mosaic dispensations, they yet all are different ages of the same church: the same substantial principles, both of justice and grace, belong to them all: and the changes are changes of form and development. Accordingly we look in vain among the entire teachings of Christ to find one word uttered against the Old Testament Scriptures. When Christ came—the greatest and plainest of teachers—he found these writings in the possession of the Jews; and it is a great thing for all succeeding times to know that he gave to them the full sanction of his approval. This approval is both negative and positive; in what he did not say, and in what he did say. He found among the Jews many corruptions; and he did not fail to rebuke them plainly and boldly. They had perverted many precepts, and he corrected their errors. They had added things, and he rejected the additions. But they held these books in the most profound reverence; they esteemed them as of Divine inspiration; they reckoned the very points and letters to make each copy as correct as possible; and he never, on the one hand, charged them with having failed in their duty towards the sacred text as to its preservation; nor, on the other hand, intimated that there was any thing undue or superstitious in the veneration they paid to these ancient Scriptures. If we had nothing else, the silence of Jesus Christ would be enough to maintain among his disciples the same veneration for the Old Testament which the Jews of his day showed.

But his approbation was positive also. As he never intimates that these writings were held in undue estimation, or were about to lose the estimation in which they had been so long held, so he himself puts upon them the same esteem. He read these Scriptures publicly in the hearing of the people; he appealed to them as establishing his own claims; he enjoined upon his hearers to read them, without a qualifying word to suggest their waning influence; he constantly assumes the entire correctness of all their teachings; he declares that the Scriptures cannot be broken; and, in fact, he builds upon the narratives, and laws, and doctrines of the Old Testament, the entire structure of the New Testament Church. It is a statement not too strong by a single word to affirm, that the Old Testament writings, as they were held in the hands of the Jews in the days of Jesus Christ, have the entire sanction of his approbation and authority.

And, indeed, if the statement fails, it rather does so in understating the truth. Not only may we challenge any man to point out in the words of Christ Jesus, a single declaration that weakens the authority of these Scriptures; not only may we affirm that the New Testament would be an incomplete and fragmentary volume in the absence of the Old; but we may very plainly see that the Old Testament is a more instructive volume to us than even it was to the former ages. We may understand every important thing better than they did, and this almost in the same sense that an advanced scholar understands the rudiments of any science better than one who is learning the same things for the first time. Many truths were clearly taught them, as even Jesus Christ gives us no other moral law than that which found so clear an exhibition in the two stone tables of Sinai. The Decalogue, therefore, stands, and will stand, while time lasts, the unchanging expression of human duty. Many things were taught them by types and shadows. But we can look on these—for example, the sacrifice offered by Abel, the Brazen Serpent, or the High Priest's Entrance behind the Veil of the Tabernacle—and learn quite as much of their spiritual import as did they whose eyes actually looked upon these things. Many wonderful sights were granted to them; but the bush of the desert burning yet unconsumed; the fire from Jehovah's altar touching the prophet's lips; the exposure of three young men to a fiery furnace without injury, are lessons as useful in our times, as in the days of Moses, or Isaiah, or Daniel. They had many prophetic declarations which are clearer to us, because fulfilled. It is always the case in human affairs, that the lessons of history are better understood after they are past than while they are passing. It is true, that the things now occurring upon the earth will be better understood by our successors than we can understand them. Far more fully is it true, that we can understand the teachings of Old Testament times and Old Testament prophets better than they did, who lived, before time and succeeding revelations had cleared up its obscurities. But in this conclusion we may rest, that the New Testament does not supersede the Old; it fills it with new meaning; it makes it a more interesting book than ever before; and we will most honour Christ, when we most deeply study and most fully understand Moses and the prophets.

Among all the things written in old times "for our learning, that we through patience and comfort of the Scriptures might have hope," Rom. xv. 4; our attention seems especially called to the lessons of religious experience which these writings contain. In a remarkable degree the Scriptures abound in brief biographical sketches; the writers of the New Testament repeatedly refer to these and draw lessons from them, as if they would bind both parts of the Sacred Book together in one permanent volume; and the interest which men naturally take in such writings, has confirmed our faith in the wisdom of the inspired writers. From no kind of teaching do men usually learn more than from narratives, or biography, embodying important principles. Nor need we suppose that an example must be thoroughly good in order to be profitable. On the contrary, the mistakes of good men, the sins of men from whom we had expected better things, and the corruptions of the vilest men may be instructive as matters of record, if only we are clearly able to recognize the right and wrong as such. All past history owes its importance to the truth, that the men of former times were just such men as we ourselves are; possessing like minds, influenced by like motives, and subject to like passions. We can make allowance for the circumstantial differences of age, intelligence, cultivation, and necessity; but human nature has been ever the same. So in the lessons of the Old Testament, man has ever been the same, and the operations of Divine grace to renew and sanctify the soul, have been the same. The difference between one age and another is circumstantial; the agreement is substantial. The same God, the same law, the same grace, the same sinfulness, have been known from Adam until now; and the superior clearness with which we read these lessons, cannot make false what was formerly true, nor useless what once was profitable. It is just, then, for us to look upon the generations of past time and to learn from them the same lessons we learn from living men. There is no such difference in the nature of man, no such change in the dealings of God, as can make obsolete the teachings aforetime given to instruct the Church. It is, rather, our superior advantage to learn lessons from the entire Bible—the Old and New Testaments—having the same God for their Author, the same truth for their contents; consistent in all their teachings, purifying in all their tendencies.

CHAPTER II.

OLD TESTAMENT BIOGRAPHIES.

"Part not with these old names. See how they shine
In these old heavens, like stars, whose rays no age
Can dim, nor boastful art of man supplant
By lights, the invention of his fruitful skill."

BONAR.

THE current proverb, Example is more powerful than precept, applies as well to former ages as to present times. Men always take less interest in abstract principles than they do in the character formed upon such principles, and the conduct flowing from them. History and biography are merely the written examples of former times. Thus only can we have any faithful knowledge of those who have passed off the stage of action. We cannot see them. They are gone. But we can learn of them through the written page; we can almost recall their times and scenes; and all the generations past, though dead, yet speak to us. It is important that we should learn to interpret properly the lessons they impart. We must look upon these men of the past, just as we now think and judge of men that are living. Bad men live around us, and bad men have lived before us. Even their examples may be profitable, if we see their wrong and shun it. Good men have now, and always have had, their imperfections and their sins, often amounting to the most lamentable departures from truth and duty. We may still say with Solomon, "there is not,"— and one illustrious example excepted—there has not been, "a just man upon earth, that doeth good and sinneth not." All faithful biography is the biography of men of like passions with ourselves; of men in like circumstances, trials, and temptations. We want to see them, therefore, just as they were; or just as we would see them, if they lived and moved around us. We have often heard it said, that the best daguerreotypes are those where a man has come before the artist in his every-day clothes, and taken his seat carelessly without much thought upon the matter. It is easy to see why this is so. We get our friend as we are accustomed to see him, and everything is natural. But when a man dresses himself carefully, puts himself in his best position, and tries to appear to the best advantage, we get a picture just like that—for the instrument is faithful— but still it is stately and artificial, not at all a just likeness of the man we usually see. The great fault of the writers of biography is just like this. They usually become eulogists. They palliate the faults, and magnify the virtues of their heroes. They dress them in fine clothes, and put them in artificial positions. If there is a scar on the cheek, they give you a side view; if he is lame, they avoid a full length picture. You see the man as he appears before the artist, and not as he has been wont to appear before the world. But take the flour off the miller, and the leather apron off the blacksmith, and you hardly recognize them.

The Bible is a book of biography, because infinite wisdom has adapted it to our instruction. But we ought not to suppose that the characters of men as recorded in the Bible are any better than those recorded in other books. From the remarks just made, we ought to expect that they would be rather worse than in ordinary biographies. For if these writers are divinely inspired, they must tell us the truth, and in its plainest forms. Let us not take up the idea that infallibility of truth in the record implies that the words and conduct recorded must therefore be correct. Let us rather judge that these sacred writers, above all others, will tell the faults as plainly as the virtues of men whose memoirs they prepare for us. It is a great mistake to make objection to the inspired volume because it records the sins of men like Adam, Noah, Abraham, and David. For the record of these sins is proof of excellency in the biographer. The Divine artist not only gives us a truthful picture, but he places the man before us in an every-day dress and attitude. Thus our idea is better of what the man was; and the effect is better for our instruction. If these men were represented as without faults, we would reject the narratives as overwrought or incredible; or we would regard them as quite out of our sphere. Just because the Bible records human history, its characters are represented as men; because they sinned, we are told they did; and the circumstances that attend their lives are just such as we should expect in their respective ages. Men who lived in a rude age are represented as rude; those who had but the dawn of revealed religion should not appear to walk in the same light which Christianity shed on the world long after they left it.

It is by no means an easy thing to decide what allowances we should justly make for the follies and errors of other ages. The law of God is unchangeable in its spirit and in its demands from age to age; and ever since God placed man upon the earth, his conscience has discerned the difference between wrong and right. And men have always known what they ought to do in some matters. Fraud, and falsehood, and impurity, and violence have never been right; and men have always known this. Wilful transgression of a known and recognized law, is to be so judged in every age. But we know very well that the consciences of men are often much influenced by the circumstances in which they are placed; and the amount of a man's guilt is increased or diminished by the light he had. One hundred years ago, men of high standing in the Christian Church engaged in the slave trade, used and sold intoxicating liquors, and stood aside from efforts to promote missions to the heathen, to an extent that would ruin the Christian reputation of any man who would do the like things now. But we judge of them with due allowance for the faults and errors of their age. It may not be an easy thing to decide how much allowance to make for such things. But we get a false view of the past, if we do not remember this. For he is a very remarkable man who rises much above the spirit of the times in which he lives.

We have said that it is more profitable for us, that the men spoken of in the Scriptures should be represented in their natural characters. We learn most when we read of men like ourselves. We are to be followers of them who through faith and patience inherit the promises. When we see that men of imperfect piety have been accepted of God, we are not utterly disheartened if our own piety is imperfect. It encourages our trials of patience that the long trials of Abraham found their reward. We sin against God; we wander from the path of duty; we need encouragement to return. How dark would be our way, how hopeless our thoughts, if there was no recorded instance of sin in any of God's children, or of his mercy shown to a backslider! In these sacred histories we read the records of our brethren; the records of God's forbearance and tender mercy; the records of just such a church as exists around us; the records that are exactly suited for every lesson of warning and encouragement, according to our necessities.

Not only are these scriptural portraits truthful, but they are placed in the right attitude; are clothed in the proper dress; and are surrounded by natural circumstances. And these things are all "written for our learning, that we through patience and comfort of the Scriptures might have hope." Rom. xv. 4.

CHAPTER III.

THE FIRST MAN.

"He, moulded by his Maker into man,
At once upstood, intelligent, surveyed
All creatures; with precision understood
Their purport, uses, properties; assigned
To each his name significant, and filled
With love and wisdom, rendered back to heaven
In praise harmonious the first air he drew."
COWPER.

THE well written life of any man might profit a serious reader. This does not mean that every man's history is equally valuable. The lives of some men possess special interest. They have held some important place in history; uttered excellent sentiments; done great things; or exerted a large influence upon their own and other generations.

In the lives of few men could mankind have a more general interest than in that of the first father of our race. It is indeed a long distance to look back to Adam. Nearly five thousand years have passed away since he laid his venerable head in the dust from which he sprung; generation after generation of his children has filled the earth with their joys and their sorrows, and has submitted to the same stroke of inexorable death. Yet Adam can never be forgotten. Even to us and to generations yet unborn, the institutions that began with Adam are passing down as blessings; and a far and deep rolling tide of the swelling waters of sorrow, let in upon us by his rash hand, has submerged all intervening generations, and shall yet dash its mighty surges against the most distant shores of time. There should be a precedence of interest to us in the life and character of the first man. If influence upon the race gives interest to the race, we should all wish to know as much as possible of Adam and of his relations to us. The recorded incidents of his life are few, though, if we reckon his adult years, we may regard his as the longest life of which we know. But the paucity of events is compensated by peculiar interest.

"Adam," says the Evangelist Luke, "was the son of God." That is, being the first of the race, he and our first mother were formed by God's direct agency. We may easily judge therefore that he was a perfect man; just what a man should be. God pronounced him very good. His body then was well formed, strong, and healthy: his mind mature, active, and even intelligent; and his affections, and his conscience ready to respond to all the holy demands of God's moral law. It seems unreasonable to think that God's crowning work of six days' creation was an overgrown child; having a man's physical powers and a child's intelligence. Adam was not helpless and dependent as an infant now is. He was finite, but he was intelligent. He knew God his Creator; he knew his relations and duties to him; and when Eve was formed, his relations and duties to her. This is what is meant when it is said, he had the law of God written upon his heart. And when we are told in the New Testament that every regenerated soul of man is renewed in knowledge after the image of Him that created him, it seems implied that man was originally created in the knowledge of his Maker.

And God made man upright. He was not only a moral being, but a holy being. God looked upon him and declared that he was very good. The works of God are good because they serve the end for which he made them. As in human affairs, a watch is good when it keeps good time, and though some watches are of more costly materials, yet every watch is good if it truly serves this end, so in Divine matters. The sun is a good creature of God when it fills the place for which God designed it; a tree is good when it brings forth the fruit it was designed to bear; and man, who was to glorify God by the holiness of his character, can be called good only when he is truly holy. As it is impossible for us to conceive of Adam as neither holy nor unholy, so we must believe that he was a holy being, as God at first created him.

And as God made man at the first, he was an

immortal creature in his whole person. We have no just reason to think that death would ever have touched man if Adam had not sinned. We do not mean by this that the lower orders of creatures would never have died; nor that Adam would have been incapable of all pain and suffering; nor that he would always have remained on earth. But the occurrence of death to beasts that have no immortal part is a different thing from its occurrence to man. Doubtless the creatures are subject to various evils through the sin of man, while yet they would have still been mortal had man never transgressed. Doubtless Adam himself, even in his estate of innocence, might have felt the pangs of hunger and fatigue, for these seem inseparable from the capacity to eat and to sleep. Doubtless also this earth was never designed for the permanent home of man. But we may judge that, after an allotted time upon the earth, Adam would have passed away in the body, as did Enoch and Elijah in after years. The fact that two men—sinful men—have left the earth without dying, is abundant proof of the possibility, that had man remained holy, this would have been the usual method of his transfer from earth to heaven. This at least is certain, that death to man is a judicial sentence, and the fruit of sin. "By one man sin entered into the world, and death by sin; and so death passed upon all men for that all have sinned." As God made Adam, he was in soul and in body an immortal creature.

Many thoughts have been uttered in the solution of this question, How was man made in the image of God? As God is a pure Spirit, so this language cannot at all refer to man's bodily form. Yet there are several things which together make up the full force of the expression. As God is a Spirit, so is man in his superior part; God is intelligent, so is man; God is ever existing, man is immortal; God is the universal ruler, man has dominion over the earth; God is holy, so was man made. And though this chief excellency of man was lost, yet man has not so lost the image of God, but that he still possesses a conscience, and remains a moral being. Sin darkens and defiles the conscience, warps its judgments, and makes its actings sluggish; and even seems almost to sear it and to destroy all healthy action. But the result of totally destroying the conscience in man, even ignorance and wickedness can never reach. Man can discern the distinction of right and wrong, and he approves and condemns himself in all he is or does. This is a distinguishing and essential characteristic; and by this man is separated from the brute creation, by an impassable barrier. Thought, memory, affection, and will, to a limited extent, brutes have; but neither have they, nor can education impart to them, a conscience.

Many misconceptions exist upon this subject, and this is a common opinion, "that if conscience is an essential part of man's nature, every conscience ought to dictate the same decisions." But even if men were placed in circumstances exactly similar, it is a mistake to suppose that conscience is the power of making infallible decisions. As man's memory is not perfect, nor his understanding always right, so his conscience is not infallible. Inform two men of the facts in any case; set them free from all bias, and let them carefully consider it; and even then they may differ in judgment. The judgments of conscience pertain to moral matters; but there is the same need of instruction, of impartiality, and of due consideration. The chief differences in the decisions of the human conscience arise from ignorance, prejudice, and passion. Certainly this would be a better world if every man would deal faithfully, and do justly, and speak truthfully as well as he might be able to do. Yet man on earth, in his best estate and in the best exercise of his powers, is still imperfect; and those who have most earnestly contended that conscience is an essential element of his mental constitution, have never affirmed or expected an entire uniformity of moral decisions.

CHAPTER IV.

ADAM IN PARADISE.

"Oh, happy pair,
Lords of fair Eden's blooming range, where earth,
Benignant parent, from her verdant lap
Spontaneous poured her bounteous sweets, and gave
Whate'er could minister delight."

HAYES.

MAN, as he came from the hands of his Creator, was a glorious and happy being. God was his Father and his Friend; and in God and in his works Adam found constant delight. In kind care for him, God planted a garden eastward in Eden. The whole earth was then beautiful. Beautiful scenery, and fruitful trees, and fragrant flowers, and joyous living things were everywhere around him.

But Eden was earth's fairest garden-spot; more beautiful for situation than other spots, more fertile, better planted, better watered. He that made man's eye knew what prospects could charm it; he that formed man's ear knew every sound of natural melody; he that gave taste to man knew what food would gratify it; and all these things, we doubt not, he gathered about the garden. The name "Eden" signifies pleasantness or pleasure; and to a contented mind this was a spot of peace and delight.

As the Scriptures use the word "Paradise" to signify that garden and also heaven itself, so, doubtless, it bore some resemblance to heaven. Life breathed in its air, life flowed in its streams, life bloomed and ripened in its fruits, life was the promised reward of its holy labours. How glorious was man in Eden; lord, but not tyrant of all; king in a realm of peace, and order, and happiness; a priest to offer sweet thanksgivings to the Almighty; no dangers threatened from disease or death; peaceful within, safe around; formed for endless honour, endless improvement, endless usefulness; angels his friends, God his visitor! And all these blessings, had Adam remained in holiness, he would have transmitted to countless millions; who, inheriting from him peace, and righteousness, and blessedness, would have held him in everlasting honour.*

Yet this perfection of man was necessarily the perfection of a finite creature. We may notice several things to show the limits of his condition.

1. Man was liable to fall. He was capable of standing, but free to sin. Absolute incapability of change belongs only to God himself. Adam, of his own nature, could not be unchangeable in holiness. Some suppose that a free creature must of necessity be liable to sin; and that even God cannot prevent a free creature from sinning. A most dreadful

* Dwight's Theology. i. 349.

doctrine, the truth of which must forbid God to promise everlasting life; and must prevent the very inhabitants of heaven from having any assurance of their continued standing! We, rather, believe that God can establish a free being in holiness and happiness. But he placed Adam in an estate of probation, with power to keep the law of God, but liable to transgress it.

2. God placed him in the garden to till the ground. Doubtless the labour of Adam before the fall, was exempt from the toilsome, laborious, and often fruitless exertion which men must often now put forth. "In the sweat of thy face thou shalt eat bread," is a part of the curse afterwards given. Labour in Paradise was occupation rather than toil; employment that was pleasant and healthful to soul and body, rather than an irksome task. And, if Adam, even then, needed labour for his happiness, let us learn that some useful occupation is far more needful now for every man, if he would be happy in the enjoyment of life, or if he would keep himself from being a useless, indeed a pernicious member of society. It is impossible for any man to be blessed in himself or a blessing to others, who has not something to do. "The great secret" of keeping the heart, says Bishop Horne, "is employment. An empty house is everybody's property. All the vagrants about the country will take up their quarters in it. Always, therefore, have something to do, and you will always have something to think

about. God has placed every person in some station, and every station has a set of duties belonging to it." Adam was not idle in Paradise; and idleness still less becomes us.

3. God put bounds upon the liberty of Adam. He was free, but not lawless. He must be reminded that he was a dependent being. Lord of all he saw, he must be reminded that he was subject to God's government. God forbade him to eat of one tree, to remind him of his subjection. This tree also notified Adam that he was liable to fall. It was a kind and a perpetual warning: "Beware, lest thou depart from God." Besides, it shows man that the highest kind of happiness is to be found in the enjoyment of God himself. Earthly things cannot satisfy the soul of man. "There was a want even in Paradise," says the excellent Boston, "so that the forbidden tree was, in effect, the hand of all creatures, pointing men away from themselves; it was the sign of emptiness, hung out before the door of creation, with this inscription, 'This is not your rest.'"*

And here we may say that if God made it a law even in Paradise, when man was yet in his innocence, that he should deny his natural appetites; if self-denial was the law of Eden, how much more proper is it for sinful man, whose appetites and passions have irregular and morbid cravings, to set due bounds to them, and even for wholesome purposes,

* Fourfold State.

to abstain from lawful indulgences! It is a sentiment of infidelity, and not of piety, that the very existence of an appetite is the Divine allowance that a man may indulge it. It never was true, even when man was holy; and it is much less true now, when man's selfish passions so often destroy himself and others. Self-denial was an element of piety in man unfallen; much more must every man now deny himself, both to mortify sin, and to do good to others. We are called unto liberty, but liberty itself must be wisely used. And we may often adopt the noble sentiment of Paul, "If meat make my brother to offend, I will eat no meat while the world stands." And it is plainly evident, from the fact that God made Adam stand back from this tree, that the self-denials required of us may be no abridgment of our pure enjoyment. Adam was perfectly happy, and might have continued so, if he had not tasted of the forbidden tree. Indeed, the service of God is true happiness and all the pleasures we think to gain by disobedience will prove delusive. And we may extend the principle further than to the things directly required of us by the commands of God. When our Lord says, "It is more blessed to give than to receive," he directs our thoughts to this important principle of our nature, that whatever pleasure we find in the gratification of ourselves is inferior in its nature and short-lived in its influence, when compared with the enjoyment we receive from efforts to do good to others. In truth, let our self-denials be of what kind they may, we receive longer and better pleasure from denying ourselves for any righteous end. If we restrain our appetites from constant indulgence, we enjoy more the gratifications we do have; and if we spend ourselves or our substance in doing good to others, we have the highest pleasure in reflecting upon this.

CHAPTER V.

THE GARDEN AND ITS TREES.

"It was a place
Chosen by the sovereign planter when he formed
All things to man's delightful use."

MILTON.

MANY opinions have been formed respecting the situation of the garden of Eden, and it might gratify curiosity, but it would secure very little profit, to consider these at any length. Yet this brief statement may be made, that the site of the garden has been variously fixed in every quarter of the globe, and even outside of the globe. Some have indeed supposed, that all the landmarks of the ancient world were obliterated by the flood; and that therefore it is in vain that we attempt to identify the spot from the description in Genesis. Others judge, that the Jewish historian speaks of the rivers and the surrounding country as they existed when he wrote; and that therefore we may attempt to find the situation of the garden. Doubtless the deluge did make great changes in the channels of rivers and in the face of the country in various ways; yet we may reasonably suppose that the historian designs to give information by his terms of description. But those who so understand Moses, have had no agreement among themselves. In all the four quarters of the earth; in Syria, Babylonia, Tartary, China, Austria, Palestine, Mesopotamia, Armenia, Ceylon, Ethiopia, Prussia, Norway, and Siberia, has the site of the garden been fixed by various persons; and some, according to the testimony of Dr. Adam Clarke, have even placed it within the orbit of the moon, or in the moon itself. The celebrated Cardinal Bellarmine held the opinion that the garden of Eden yet exists in some unknown portion of the earth; and that there Enoch and Elijah were taken when they were carried away in the body: but this view was not adopted by the theologians of even his own church.* But it is not needful to pursue this matter.

The opinion most generally adopted, as agreeable to a reasonable view of the scriptural testimony, is, that Paradise was situated in Armenia; and that Moses designs to point out the well-known rivers, Tigris and Euphrates, as the streams that watered the garden. Yet the situation is, after all, of very little importance; and the conjectures of learned men serve rather to throw perplexity upon the matter than to settle the simple question.

But whatever may have been the size or the position of the garden, it was a Paradise planted by

* See Turrettine, i. 528

God for the happy abode of man. And God placed in it every tree that could add beauty to the scenery or provide food for man. We need not be surprised that Adam should live entirely upon vegetable food, or that there is no evidence of the use of animal food in the early ages. In the most densely inhabited parts of the earth even now, animal food is little used. Populous nations live entirely on the fruits of the earth. It is forbidden by the religion of some tribes to take life; and only in the coldest climates does the use of flesh seem a necessity. A grant was made to Noah to use the flesh of animals, accompanied by a restriction, which, we believe upon New Testament authority, is still in force, that no blood should be eaten. (Compare Gen. ix. 4, with Acts xv. 29.) To Adam the fruits of the earth were for food.

So the large and fruitful garden was filled with every kind of food for the support and the healthful gratification of its happy occupants. Fields of cereals waved in the summer's wind; heavy ladened boughs of mellow fruits hung within their reach; vines ran along the ground or climbed up to hang their tempting clusters on the friendly trees; and each season provided its variety and abundance, that man might eat for himself, or might enjoy the happiness which the creatures around him received from the full bounty of their common Creator.

Special mention is made of two trees in Eden. The tree of life grew in the midst of the garden;

and there was also the tree of knowledge of good and evil. It is needless to inquire whether two species, or two single trees are meant; nor need we do more than mention a few opinions as to the nature of the trees. The tree of knowledge of good and evil, the Mohammedans declare was wheat; Christians generally take it for an apple; some Jews say the vine, and others the fig, and add that from its leaves our first parents made aprons to cover their nakedness. This much only we know, that this tree was of beautiful appearance, and its fruit could be eaten. God gave it a place in Eden for the trial of man's obedience; to remind him of his subjection; to warn him of his liability to fall; and to point him to himself as the true source of his enjoyment. The influence upon man was moral. It was true then as always, "Not that which entereth into the mouth defileth the man." By God's appointment this tree indicated man's moral condition. If he obeyed God and refrained from the tree, he knew the benefits of obedience; if he transgressed, he knew the evils of disobedience. The whole account is to be taken, not as an allegory, but as a sacramental record. The tree was an external sign of things spiritual. So has God ever taught man, both before and since the fall. The name of the tree gave solemn warning of that experimental acquaintance with evil that would surely follow his partaking of it: the tree was placed before his eyes to show that man was free to stand or fall upon his own choice; while the fact that there was but a single tree, surrounded by so large an abundance, made the inducement to trangress God's will as slight as any scene of probation could make it.

The tree of life was, doubtless, also sacramental. We cannot judge that the physical virtues of any food could bestow everlasting life. This tree was a sign and symbol of life to obedient man. This tree is elsewhere mentioned in the Bible; and is said to be also in the Paradise of God above. There are not wanting reasons for believing that the tree of life was a symbol of our Lord Jesus Christ. Unfallen man did not, indeed, need him as a Mediator or a Saviour, but the Second Person of the Godhead was not unknown in Eden. Christ is the true tree of life to sinners; but we find no access if we come in the same way, and with the same hopes, as Adam. So long as man was innocent, he had free access to life; but as sinners we must approach in penitence and faith, through the new and living way opened up to us. Heb. x. 19, 20.

CHAPTER VI.

MARRIAGE AS GIVEN IN EDEN.

"Across the threshold led,
And every tear kissed off as soon as shed,
His house she enters; there to be a light
Shining within, when all without is night;
A guardian angel o'er his life presiding,
Doubling his pleasures and his cares dividing."
ROGERS.

THE first institution of social life was the ordinance of Marriage; and God has added none since of greater importance, for the purity, usefulness, and comfort of the race. And the fact, that the subject of marriage,—its importance, influence, and obligations, is not often made the theme of deliberate instruction, may justify its larger consideration on these pages than would otherwise seem suitable. It seems certainly true, that more things are deliberately said, in our communities, against the true ordinance of marriage, than should be allowed to pass without rebuke; and yet the chief instructions given are casual and incidental, rather than chosen and well-considered. Doubtless there are persons of mature age among us, who can say that they have never listened to a single public discourse, that was designed to explain this Divine ordinance. Yet surely there have been corruptions enough, from the earliest ages, from the vile passions of men, from infidelity, and even from the deliberate expression of religious tenets, to call forth just expositions of the law of God upon this especial point. It is of the greatest importance to human welfare, that just views of marriage should be entertained. and we do not need to go beyond the record in Genesis, to receive the most important hints upon the subject; though, indeed, it will be wise for us, to interpret these simple statements by the further light thrown upon them in all the word of God.

It is a great thing to know, in the beginning of our thoughts, that marriage is an ordinance of God. The Divine Creator having made man, and placed him upon the earth, thought it not good that he should be alone. So he caused a deep sleep to fall upon Adam, and from a rib of his side he formed Eve, the first woman, and brought her to the man, and Adam received her as his wife. And not only was marriage thus instituted by God, in man's primeval age of innocence, but when the glorious Son of God,—who, even in Paradise, was the Revealer of the Godhead,—appeared on earth in our nature, he gave his personal public attendance at a marriage in Cana of Galilee, and took occasion to work there the first of that splendid series of miracles, by which he proved himself the Messiah of God.* This is the first great thought upon the subject: Marriage is no device of human expediency, to be taken up, or thrown off, at the whim of man. It is an ordinance of God; only properly assumed, when regard is had to his will; only properly maintained, when the laws which he has given for it are known and regarded.

The Scriptures teach us, here and elsewhere, that marriage is to be between one man and one woman. Human iniquity, in many lands, and for many ages, has corrupted this arrangement. Instances have been known, where one woman has been the wife of many husbands.† Far more frequently, one man has been the husband of many wives. And it seems far more strange to know that this great departure from the original ordinance was tolerated, for many ages, even in the Church of God, and in the families of patriarchs and prophets. But man's utmost neglect or transgression of God's ordinances has no effect to change the law itself, or to release man from his obligations. The first record of direct opposition to the polygamy of the old dispensation, we read in the prophecies of Malachi. He not only maintains the true law of marriage, but declares that the training of the families of men in godliness,

* James's Family Monitor, chap. i.

† J. C. Lowrie's two years in India, 222. Schlegel says it is legally established among the Buddhists. Phil. of Hist. Lect. III. See also Grote's Greece, ii. 386.

was the design of God, in ordering that a man should have but one wife. It would seem that through the expostulations of this prophet, a reformation had been wrought among the Jewish people. For though polygamy belonged to every period of the Old Testament history, from the times of the patriarchs, we find not a trace of it in Judea in the New Testament times. The teachings of our Lord Jesus Christ are express upon this subject. He declares that Moses tolerated a departure from the law as originally given, because of the hardness of the hearts of men; but that in the beginning God ordained marriage for a single pair. Because of this exposition from the lips of Christ, this has remained, ever since, the teaching of the Christian Church.

From the account here given, we may learn, that marriage is properly founded upon the mutual affection of the parties, and is designed for their mutual benefit. God said it was not good for man to be alone; and he would make for him a helper, his counterpart.

There are several matters we may notice in the language of judicious commentators, who have remarked upon them. Dr. Scott says, "Eve was taken from Adam, not from the ground, that there might be a natural foundation of moderate subordination on the woman's part, and sympathizing tenderness on the man's: as a man rules over, yet carefully defends and tenderly takes care of his own body." So Matthew Henry, with forcible quaintness, says: "The woman was made of a rib out of the side of Adam; not out of his head to top him; nor out of his feet to be trampled on by him; but out of his side to be equal with him: under his arm, to be protected; near his heart, to be beloved." Nor can we easily exhaust the meaning of the word, a help-meet. It does not mean that Eve was another self for Adam. But it is wisely ordered by Providence, that the very differences of natural constitution between the sexes, should serve for mutual benefit. Man has his strength, woman has hers; man his weaknesses, and woman hers: and they are all the better adapted to be mutual helpers, because they are not alike. Doubtless our readers are familiar with a beautiful passage in the writings of Washington Irving, which has been often quoted, in which he speaks of the influence of a wife to sustain her husband in times of dejection and adversity; aptly and finely comparing her to a vine that clasps its tendrils around a sturdy tree, and climbs up upon its strength; and then when the lightning has stricken and splintered the tree, the vine seems to bind it together, and to support in turn, where it has been supported. And there can be no doubt in any thoughtful mind, that a happy marriage makes both parties more valuable members of society. There is a sense in which a man who marries is less independent than before; but he has thus lost a feeling he ought never to have cherished; and for this very reason he is more to be depended upon. Such a man now has others to care for besides himself. He has too much at stake, he has too many feelings beside his own to consult, he has too many interests besides his own to secure, to allow him to make reckless movements, or to permit him to be careless of things that affect the welfare of society.

Few things are more important for the formation of a just character, and the proper discharge of our duties, than a sense of our personal responsibility. In many respects this is better felt in this relation than ever otherwise. The experience which grows out of the family relation is needful to form a symmetrical character. On the one hand, there are energies brought out for the maintenance and comfort of the household, and there is an economical and proper application of the resources, such as we do not usually see where the motives are wanting, which the family relation supplies; and on the other hand, it is only in the family that we learn to exercise those affections and sympathies that are so much needed in a world like this. Truly we may repeat the words of Paradise, "It is not good for man to be alone." By the virtues it originates and fosters, we may recognize marriage as a kind ordination of God for the preservation, the usefulness, and the comfort of the race.

And surely this record bears upon its face the testimony which Paul only more clearly gives us afterwards, that marriage, thus ordained by God for the good of man, is honourable in all. By this is not meant that it is obligatory upon all without exception; for circumstances may fully justify individuals in remaining unmarried; there may be times of perilous persecution, when an apostle, who even then does not venture to forbid marriage, may pronounce it, for the present distress, inexpedient; and there may be persons who can rightfully purpose to live single.

But the Scriptures regard this institution as so important, that no unwise restrictions are laid upon it; the estate is holy and honourable. Long before this, had celibacy been regarded, in some portions of the world, as a peculiar privilege and a holy duty. Among the Egyptians, the priests of Isis were bound to live unmarried; in the East, celibacy was honoured; and both the Persians and the Romans had their vestal virgins, consecrated to their respective idolatries. Perhaps the apostle's words refer to these; perhaps he looked forward, by the prophetic vision, to greater corruptions, yet to be introduced into the Christian Church. "Forbidding to marry" is one of the Scriptural marks of departure from the faith, and is especially mentioned by the same apostle, when he would foretell the rise and characteristics and fall of the Church of Rome. And the fulfilment of his words, thus far, may be seen in the prohibitions of that apostate Church, against the marriage of her clergy, and other religious orders;

and the wisdom of the Scriptural rule is proved by the miserable results of priestly celibacy for ages. The standing of the Romish Church, upon the subject of marriage, is like her position upon many other matters. The professions of that body are, in many things, almost as near right as possible; and yet she may have professions, and has practice abundant, in the same matters, directly contrary to right. Theoretically, she has but one God; practically, she has many; theoretically, God alone receives true worship; practically, more prayers are addressed to the Virgin Mary than to Christ; theoretically, almost every orthodox doctrine can be found in her creed; practically, her councils and her teachers have introduced an amazing number of important errors, to obscure the truth, to cover it over, and to prevent its wholesome influence. Upon the subject of marriage, the Romish Church exerts a wholesome influence, in a single respect, that the tie is rendered permanent, and almost indissoluble; but here also appear the contradictory teachings, so characteristic of her. On the one hand, she affirms that marriage is a solemn sacrament, instituted by Christ, and pronounces a fearful curse upon all who deny this; and on the other hand, she peremptorily forbids marriage to all her priesthood, and in the face of all her members, extols the virtue of perpetual chastity, encourages vows for this end, erects monasteries and nunneries, and fills them with those that are forbidden to marry, and regards these persons as only the more holy, because they have refrained from the use of this sacrament of the house of God!

Now directly in opposition to the existing corruptions of idolatrous nations all around him, and to the prospective corruptions of the great apostasy before him, the Apostle Paul returns to the original law of Eden, and declares that "marriage is honourable in all." And it is the only effectual preservative of human happiness and human purity. Individual persons, through natural disposition, or by the force of righteous principles, may live in purity and usefulness without marriage; but calamitous experience has abundantly proved, that no large class of persons, taken indiscriminately from human society, can be bound to celibacy, without producing a state of morals the most miserable and corrupt. Prophecy foretells these evils in the Church of Rome; history has written their dark records; and their gloomy shadows fall now upon every land where that is the prevailing faith. The true and wholesome doctrine is, that marriage is sacred, but not a sacrament; sacred in this sense, that its vows are inviolable; sacred in this, that God will judge all that break these solemn obligations; and sacred, that it subserves the most valuable ends to promote righteousness in the earth. How well does our great English poet describe it:

"By it
Founded in reason, loyal, just, and pure,
Relations dear, and all the charities
Of father, son, and brother first were known;
Far be it that we should write it sin or blame,
Or think it unbefitting holiest place,
Perpetual fountain of domestic sweets."*

But these thoughts would be too lamentably imperfect, and especially, alas! too inapplicable to growing evils in our times, without adding this important principle, that marriage is designed by God to be a *permanent* relationship. There is virtually, by Divine permission, a severing of the ties that have bound us to an endeared home, from our childhood up; and one man and one woman, coming forth from their several parental homes, solemnly vow to cleave to each other, leaving all others for each other, forming a new family in the earth, and declaring that death only shall separate them. So runs the original record: "Therefore shall a man leave his father and his mother, and shall cleave unto his wife, and they shall be one flesh." That is, by the covenant of marriage, through the ordinance of God, a man and his wife become kindred to each other; a relationship is formed, as true, and more tender and intimate than that between a parent and a child; and it can never be sundered, but by the death of one party, or by guilt which God will avenge. Henceforward these parties are to love each other as their ownselves.

* Paradise Lost, iv. 755.

It is quite impossible, indeed, that their views and wishes should be always alike. However congenial their tempers, or however happy their union, no two persons can live long together without differing in their judgments and desires; and we may expect these differences to be more frequent and greater, because of the imperfections and the sinfulness of our nature, as now fallen.

Marriage does not overlook these things, but is wisely adapted to soften down the roughness of our characters. And mutual forbearance, and mutual affection, and a common purpose to serve the same God, and a common interest in the temporal and spiritual prosperity of the household, and a wise regard to the Divine purposes in the discipline of life, can even make these diversities work together for mutual happiness and mutual benefit. No wise parties expect to find perfection in each other, and these solemn vows are made with the full knowledge that forbearance will be called for. The scriptural rule to regulate the whole matter is love. Let a man love his wife even as himself. Some things are not necessarily included in the love a man has for his own body. A man does not need to believe that he has a strong body, or a beautiful body, or a healthy body; but it is his body, and he nourishes, and cherishes, and loves it as such. And if it be true that a man's true love for his wife will make him sometimes blind to her imperfections, and always lenient to them,—for charity thinketh no evil,—it is still also true that a man is bound to cherish his wife, that a woman is bound to love her husband, even as their ownselves, when the warmest affection cannot overlook most grievous and serious deficiencies. It is manifest that the severest tests of conjugal affection are not found in those evils which we class among the imperfections of our nature. Sin, which renders the law of marriage more needful, has brought in, also, many and severer tests to try its strength. When these parties, in the bloom and promise of their youth, stand together, before the God who made them, and surrounded by a circle of affectionate friends, who are all to be drawn nearer together by these new cords of love, who can possibly foretell the events that lie in their common pathway for perhaps fifty years in advance! How many changes in views, in conduct, in character, may a brief period reveal? The poor may become rich, or the rich poor; strength may change to weakness, health to disease, and cheerfulness to fretful repinings. But these are not the worst changes. The bright morning of wedded life, dawning without a cloud, and with the cheerful melody of nature's sweetest harmonies, has too often, before noon, clouded over with the dark shadows, through which even hope can scarcely look, beneath whose muttering thunders every happy song is silenced, and from which the setting of life's sun is often a relief. How often, in the sad experience of many a happy household, has Intemperance, like the subtle serpent, gliding into Paradise for the ruin of the first family of man, entered into the Eden where youth and virtue dwelt, to present those attractive and dangerous indulgences that have no better symbol than in the first forbidden tree. But it is not needful, in our present thoughts, to describe the evils that do sometimes spring up in earthly households, that cannot be wholly anticipated by the wisest foresight, and that the warmest affection cannot ward off. Justice requires us to say that marriage does more to keep such evils from springing up, and to repress and to correct them, than any other influence exerted in society. But when either party becomes idle, improvident, or vicious, there is the same duty incumbent upon the other party to forbear with them, and to follow them with earnest and affectionate efforts to reclaim their declining steps, which is universally recognized as the duty of parents toward erring children. How deep is the grief of a fond father and a tender mother for the wanderings of a beloved son! How long do they refuse to believe the proofs of guilt that are too plain for other eyes! what sacrifices of time, and money, and feelings will they not make, while there is any hope of reformation! how kindly do they interpret the feeblest kindlings of repentance! and how thankfully do they receive the returning prodigal to their warmest embraces! But the relation of husband and wife is more close and tender than that of parent and child. These parties have left their parents for each other: and it is the natural order of Providence that their children shall leave them, and then they are still to cleave to each other. In this world of sin this tie must hold, not to apologize for sin, or to make a common cause for its promotion, but to clog the footsteps of the sinner, and by love's strong influences to draw him back, if possible, to the paths of virtue. The wilful, resolute, irreparable separation of one party, leaves the other free to seek by proper means a dissolution of the bond: especially unfaithfulness to marriage engagements is a just ground for divorce: but apart from these two things, the covenant of marriage is not to be broken by any calamities providentially occurring to either, by any misconduct not involving a breach of the marriage law, nor by any difficulties between the parties, the most numerous, and serious, and onerous to bear. As a man cherishes his own body, though sometimes his flesh becomes feeble and diseased, and even loathsome, because it is his body, so must these parties love and cherish each other. It is a great trust which one human being commits to another, when these mutual pledges of lifelong love are made.

Many may feel disposed to say, as even the disciples of Christ said when their Lord gave just such teachings, "If the case of a man be so with his wife, it is good not to marry." Matt. xix. 10. But a juster and wiser view of the great interests of society, and of the actual workings of Providence, will vindicate the Divine rule. Facts will prove that where the Divine law is regarded, the marriage relation is usually happy. We wonder to see the changes it makes; transforming the timid, trifling, volatile girl into the self-possessed, dignified, useful matron; changing the pleasure-loving, reckless man into the provident, thoughtful, conservative citizen. And it is so important for the training and happiness of the children, for the comfort and usefulness of the parties themselves; and for the purity and well-being of society, that marriage should be indissoluble; the amount of wretchedness that must come in upon the innocent and the guilty in every case of separation is so great; the cases are so numerous where the sacredness of the relation tends to settle the difficulties that might otherwise become serious; the cases are so rare in comparison where plausible reasons for a separation can be found, that the only safe and proper ground for the relation is that taken in the Scriptures. If to consider this tie as indissoluble, makes it a more serious thing to assume the vows of marriage; if more serious thoughts should precede engagements of this nature; if a more thorough acquaintance with each other should be thought wise in those who are to be united for life; and if a true affection for each other is the only proper basis of such a union; surely these tendencies are eminently for the good of the parties and of society. We may easily judge that Divine wisdom designed that such influences should flow from his ordinance.

The value of the Scriptural ordinance of marriage may appear from the virulence with which wickedness has opposed and perverted it. Human corruption cannot spread widely without perverting marriage. The first result is the degradation of the female sex; for though it is true, that woman always drags man down with her when she falls, it is also true that the heaviest curses of corruption of manners and of civil misrule, always fall on her hapless head. The condition of woman in all lands where the Bible is not, is itself a sufficient vindication that a kind and holy God has given man these sacred writings. Well might the Indian women of New England, two hundred years ago, look upon John Elliot as almost an angel; and the Caffres of South Africa call the missionary "The shield of woman." "Really," said a Hindu female recently to a Christian lady, "your Bible must have been written by a woman, it contains so many kind things about us; our Shasters say nothing of us but what is hard and cruel."* Except Christianity, every system of religion on earth degrades and oppresses the female sex. Paganism makes woman the slave of her husband while he lives, and strangles her, or burns her, or makes her an outcast when he dies. Buddhism, Mahommedanism, and Hinduism deny that she has a soul, and pronounce

* Foreign Missionary, 22, 388.

her irreclaimably wicked. Talmudic Judaism, when not placed in contact with Christianity, leaves her without instruction;* and subtle Infidelity, with the grossest flattery of the sex, and the avowed advocacy of Woman's Rights, always unsexes, degrades, and demoralizes her. Take the world at large, and the bondage of woman, except the prevalence of irreligion from which it springs, is by far the worst social evil of the race. The Bible alone exerts an influence to make woman truly free; raises her from her degradation; speaks words of kindness in all her trials, and in the hour of her deepest bereavement cheers her eyes with the precious promises, that in all its pages speak of the widow's God, as the stars of heaven shine, numerous and bright, when darkness covers the earth.

Well may the women of Christian lands fill our churches and rally around the Bible. They owe to it their temporal comforts as well as their religious hopes. Well may they suspect any flattering talk about their rights, which places them in any other position than that assigned to them in the Bible. Let them know all this talk, from the pernicious fruits of infidelity and licentiousness which it early and surely brings forth. The women of Christian lands have nothing to hope from infidelity. And for the well-being of all society, as well as for the special welfare of the female sex, it is a matter of vital importance that the ordinance of marriage be

* Miss. Herald, 1850, 146.

maintained as God gave it to Adam in Paradise, and as it is explained upon the subsequent pages of the sacred volume. We should regard these as crying and pernicious evils of our times: that the peace of families is held in too low estimate; that differences which should be settled in the household are so easily magnified, and so readily given to the public ear; that so many instances of desertion and of unfaithfulness to marriage vows are given with all their loathsome details in the public prints; and, worse than all, that our legislators and our courts of law lend their influence, too often, to demoralize the country, by their lenient judgments upon licentious crimes, and especially by the facility with which divorces are decreed without the semblance of a fair investigation, and for the most frivolous reasons. Nor should we omit to say, that these things are made worse by the thoughtlessness of people, who, in their serious moments, know better and feel better. These allow themselves to speak too freely of other families; to talk too lightly of the remedies which aggrieved parties should seek, and to express a confident and mischievous judgment in cases with which they have but a slight and partial acquaintance.

Happy is the people where the ordinance of marriage is maintained as God gave it to our first parents. Happy is the married pair who are joined with the approbation and blessing of the almighty God; who love each other as their ownselves; and who, in the beautiful figure of one of Burns's Scottish songs, climb life's hill in company; press hand in hand down its further slope, and sleep together at the foot. Many eventful scenes will, indeed, occur between the starting and the resting spot; perhaps a separating hour comes early, and one is left to pass onward in life alone. We know not how this was with Adam; for the length of Eve's life is not recorded. But we are led to infer that they grew old together, and saw the increase of their children around them. We can know some of their griefs and some of their joys. The patrimony of their Father they soon lost; and bankrupt in character, and bankrupt in fortunes, they went forth from that delightful garden to toil in a world which their sin had cursed. What sorrows had they in the murder of one child by the hand of another! what mingled grief and joy in their own sins as contrasted with the tokens of Divine forgiveness; in the piety of Abel, and in the impiety of Cain! Life passed with them, as it passes with their children, with all its varieties of care and comfort, of peace and perplexity, of hope and fear.

Supposing that they grew old together, what a life was theirs! The first married pair started life together, and spent nearly nine centuries and a half in their companionship. What a patriarchal scene! How much must they have grown in attachment to each other! How much was there of mutual dependence; a delightful leaning upon each other, and deriving their happiness from each other! And from the days of their declining age to this, earth has no more venerable sight than is presented by an aged couple, who have gone through life together, have settled their children in the earth, and draw near the end of their days with the respect and love of all that know them.

Yet this one thing is needful to complete the picture: that they have trained up a *godly household;* that they have sent forth their children to bless the land; and that having served God and their generation here, they are only waiting for his summons to depart to that better country, where, indeed, "there is neither marrying nor giving in marriage," but where love shall abide for ever, and separations never be known.

Only waiting till the shadows
  Fall a little longer;
Waiting while their hopes of heaven
  Firmer grow, and stronger;
Watching, as the tabernacle
  Of this flesh is falling;
Judging each new imperfection
  Is their Father calling.

Trusting, that through death's cold river,
  Christ their Lord will guide them;
Praying that its narrow waters
  May not long divide them.
Lingering thus, to earth and heaven
  Warm affections bind them;
Hoping blessings, leaving blessings,
  For the loved behind them.

Blessed is the land whose children are joined in these sacred and permanent ties, and where righteous parents train up their households in the fear of God, and in a blessed looking for immortality. The hopes of our country largely rest on the pure and pious maintenance of the family relation, as God formed it in Paradise. Depart in any measure from this; let the tie of marriage be thoughtlessly formed, or thoughts of its dissolution be readily entertained, or separations be esteemed reputable; and woe to the parties, to their offspring, and to society! A mutual lifelong interest in their children, demands that parents should have a lifelong interest in each other. And it is chiefly because the children of the human family need a moral training extending through twenty years, and because this usually determines the character for our everlasting existence, that this ordinance is so divinely appointed. The Lord seeks a godly seed; that is, the family, as he has formed it, is a religious institution; and fearful guilt belongs to those who venture to pervert it from this design. And they who form their families after the Divine design, may hope for even a greater permanence than belongs to a lifelong covenant. The most precious hope for a family is in these things: that its members are fitted for God's service here and hereafter; that his favour is chiefly sought in all they do and are; that the separations that must occur will be only for a little season; and that, not long hence, the whole family shall meet together around the throne of God.

There is a coming day when no remembered scenes of our earthly homes will be recalled with more pleasure than that described in the familiar verse of Burns:

"Then kneeling down to heaven's eternal King,
The saint, the father, and the husband prays;
Hope springs exulting on triumphant wing,
That thus they all shall meet in future days,
There ever bask in uncreated rays,
No more to sigh or shed the bitter tear,
Together hymning their Creator's praise,
In such society, yet still more dear,
While circling time moves round in an eternal sphere."

CHAPTER VII.

THE ORIGIN AND PERPETUITY OF THE SABBATH.

"Hail to the day, which He who made the heaven,
Earth, and their armies, sanctified and blest,
Perpetual memory of the Maker's rest!
Hail to the day, when He, by whom was given
New life to man, the tomb asunder riven,
Arose! That day his church hath still confest,
At once Creation's and Redemption's feast,
Sign of a world called forth, a world forgiven."

BP. MANT.

THE institution of the Sabbath is another of the ordinances of Eden. Mention is made of it in the first chapter of Genesis; and the second chapter is a summary of the first. Doubtless Eve was created upon the same sixth day with Adam; and the next day was the first Sabbath. These two institutions of man's innocence,—marriage and the Sabbath,—were designed to be perpetual for the race. Men make a great mistake when they allow themselves to think of the Sabbath as a Jewish institution. It is not so in any just sense of the term. Doubtless Moses adopted for the Jews, by Divine direction, many laws which had been in use previously and elsewhere; and he sometimes made changes in these, adapting them to the Jewish people. So the Jews had several kinds of Sabbaths; as every seventh year was a Sabbatical year, and every seven times seven was succeeded by a year of Jubilee: and the penalties for Sabbath desecration were peculiarly Jewish. But the weekly Sabbath itself was not founded by Moses: it was in existence twenty-five hundred years before his day: and when the law was given on Sinai, the fourth commandment expressly recognized the Sabbath as an existing and ancient institution. In terms that commandment does not enact a Sabbath; but it enjoins that men should "remember" that a Sabbath already existed; and that God instituted it, when he rested from the work of creation. To abolish the ceremonial law of Moses and the entire Jewish church state, does not abolish the Sabbath, or impair its authority. As it was given to Adam in Paradise, it was plainly designed for all his children; nor are there any arguments to make the Sabbath binding upon any body or any age, that do not establish its value, propriety, and authority for all the sons of men and in every age.

The institution of the Sabbath for man, while he was in his estate of innocence, affords us a reasonable proof of its perpetual obligation. Every one can see that if marriage was necessary to man unfallen, for the preservation, purity, and comfort of the race, its importance and necessity were only increased when man became a sinner. True reasoning would urge that the more man became corrupt, the more he rebelled against the law of marriage, the greater was the necessity of maintaining the law. The sinfulness of man makes the law of marriage more needful, at the same time that it makes it more difficult to retain it in all its strictness. And so may we reason of the Sabbath-day. If sinless man needed one day in seven that he might cease his usual employments, and find time to worship God without distraction, how much more are the rest and the law of the Sabbath necessary for sinful man! It is not strange that nothing is said of the Sabbath from this time forward until the time of the going forth of the Israelites from Egypt; for the history of two thousand years is put within the brief compass of a few chapters. Yet we find Noah, Jacob, and Laban observing the week as a division of time; and the Israelites gathering double manna on the sixth day, and finding none on the seventh; and commanded to observe the Sabbath even before they came to Mount Sinai; all which are indications that though the Sabbath may have been laxly kept, as marriage degenerated into polygamy, still it was known through all the intervening period between Adam and Moses. When therefore we find the law of the Sabbath written in the midst of the ten commandments, just in the place where we would expect to find it if God designed it to be of perpetual obligation; when we see that no precept that belongs peculiarly to the Jewish dispensation received any such distinction; when we know that God wrote it twice in the moral law, and that Moses has recorded it twice in his writings, and that the reasons there given for its observance are drawn from the creation as suitable to all men, and not as elsewhere from the redemption from Egypt as suitable peculiarly to Israel;* and when we can easily see that the Sabbath is as needful and suitable for every land and every age as for any time or any people, we seem to find in all these things, reasons for regarding it as of perpetual obligation.

And the proof is far more conclusive as we pass to notice other things. We read in the prophecies of Isaiah (lvi. 6, 8), that God promises large blessings to the strangers from all nations that should join themselves to the Lord and keep his Sabbaths. As the Gentiles were not called into the Church until after the dawning of the Christian dispensation, the prophet must mean that the Sabbath was still to be a Divine institution, and still to be kept holy, and still to be a blessing to those who kept it, after the time of the calling of the Gentiles. So we read that our blessed Lord, who vindicated the Sabbath from Pharisaical notions that forbade works of mercy on that day, still teaches us that the Sabbath was made for man, for the race, everywhere and always; and speaks of it

* Compare Ex. xx. 11, with Deut. v. 15.

as obligatory, even after the setting up of the Christian Church. Matt. xxiv. 20. And when we find the disciples of Christ assembling for worship on the first day of the week, calling it the Lord's day, and transmitting it to the Christian Church to be observed ever since, in memory of the resurrection of Christ, the proof seems complete that God designed to give the Sabbath to man as an ordinance of perpetual obligation.

And it is a very great mistake for any man to suppose that the change of the day from the seventh to the first day of the week, invalidates, in any degree, the claims of the Christian Sabbath. The very reverse is true. The change of day is a certain proof that the institution remains in perpetuity. For if the Sabbath had remained for the Christian Church upon the same day that had been kept from the foundation of the world, the objection would at once arise that the Christians had adopted it merely through the force of their old prejudices. It would surely be called a Jewish ceremony transferred to the Christian Church. If we consider the circumstances of the early Christian Church—composed so largely of converts who had been educated in all the forms of Judaism, who regarded the Mosaic law as of Divine original, and who clung so closely to all of their former faith which they could possibly retain—we may easily decide that the apostles could have abolished the Sabbath altogether with more ease than they could retain the institution and change the day. If they had said that the Sabbath was to be done away with entirely—like their types and sacrifices—their converts might have acquiesced. But in a few instances Christianity gave Judàism something in exchange for the ordinances it took away; and in every such case, the very reasons for the exchange would serve to call the attention of the Church to the institutions. The altar, the priest, the type, even the temple, must pass away; for Christ has come, and men may now everywhere worship the Father. The Paschal Lamb may find its substitute in the simple supper of our Lord. But the chief substitutes which Christianity made of new ordinances for those existing in the old economy, were two; and it is remarkable that neither of them was established by Moses, but both belonged to the previous patriarchal dispensation.

For circumcision was substituted baptism; this signifies the same thing, seals the same covenant, pledges the same spiritual blessings, is applied to the same subjects, and occupies the same position. If the Jew asked the reason for making any change when the same things were meant, reasons were ready. The promised seed had come; Abraham's race needed no longer to be distinguished; and a Church for all nations needed a simpler seal of the great covenant. For the seventh-day Sabbath, Christianity substituted the first-day Sabbath; and the sufficient reason is, the Redemption by Christ is a greater thing to be commemorated in the Church of God than the creation of the world. If circumcision dates back to Abraham, the Sabbath is older yet; and Christianity is not to be charged with following Jewish laws, if it substantially retains them both. But is it not true that the very attempt to change the Sabbath from one day to another implies the intelligent agitation of the subject in the early Christian Church? and is it not true that the successful effort to make the change is proof that they acknowledged the authority by which the change was made? The unquestionable fact that Christians have observed the first day of the week as the Christian Sabbath, is entirely inconsistent with the repeal of the Sabbath law, when the institutions of Moses were abrogated. The change argues perpetuity, and a perpetuity founded upon an intelligent conviction of duty, rather than upon a formal and thoughtless adoption of an ancient prejudice.

Add to all these thoughts the deeply important argument that the blessing of God has been upon the Christian Sabbath; and the proof is complete to show that its obligation is universal and perpetual.

God long ago promised that when his house had become a house of prayer for all people, he would give his blessing upon all that would keep his Sabbaths without polluting them. Isa. lvi. 6; this promise he has fulfilled. A Sabbath-keeping people, or family, or person, is blessed. How many ruined men trace the first steps of their downfall to Sabbath-desecration! How many have found instruction, and righteousness, and peace, and salvation, by the honouring of God's Sabbath! If we have evidence of God's blessing on anything earthly, it is upon the Sabbath.

Now it is no fitting reply to proofs like these, that Paul seems to argue that the Sabbath is no longer binding. For the tenor of the Apostle's arguments confines his thoughts to the ceremonial Sabbaths of the Jewish economy; to refer his words to the weekly Sabbath would place him in contradiction to the words of the sacred writings, and to his own practice, so as Paul never is found. But the single and sufficient key by which to interpret his language may be found in this conclusive fact, that the church did not understand the great Apostle of the Gentiles as arguing against the Christian Sabbath, or as desiring that it should be abolished. If—as these modern interpreters would allege—Paul tried to break down the Sabbath, no man that ever lived could have exerted a greater influence to effect such an object. But the facts are all against the thought that he made any such attempt. The Christian church retained the fourth commandment in her decalogue as it was before; used the Sabbath for the worship of God; gave a new and striking sanction to the day by making it commemorate the resurrection of Christ, and sent it down to our own times as a perpetual proof that neither Paul nor any other inspired writer made any efforts to effect its destruction.

CHAPTER VIII.

NATURE, DESIGN, AND DUTIES OF THE SABBATH.

"Welcome that day, the day of holy peace,
The Lord's own day! to man's Creator owed,
And man's Redeemer; for the soul's increase
In sanctity and sweet repose bestowed.
Type of the rest when sin and care shall cease,
The rest remaining for the loved of God!"
BP. MANT.

THE most important question after all, especially in the times in which we live, does not respect the perpetuity of the weekly rest; but the nature, and design, and obligations of the day as a Sabbath. No thoughtful mind can well venture to question that to take away the sacred obligations of the Sabbath is to destroy all its real value. The enemies of the Sabbath have no real wish that this day of the week should be blotted from our Calendar; nor wish that it should be made a day of unremitting toil, like other days of the week. If the question was taken, Shall we have a Sabbath or no Sabbath? the votes for its entire abolition would be few indeed. Even the men who are most zealously engaged in active efforts for Sabbath desecration, would start back from the consequences of taking away the day, and of making it like the other days of the week. The busy railroads in and near our large cities; the places of resort and amusement; the saloons and the drinking houses, find the Sabbath their most profitable day: and these, and thousands with them, who put forth every exertion that interest and a hatred to religion can prompt, to secure the most abundant Sabbath desecration on every hand, would yet not touch the burden with one of their fingers, if the question was purely for the abolition of the Sabbath. The enemies of the Sabbath do not meet the question fairly. They want a Sabbath, but they wish unbounded license upon it: just as the mass of ungodly men would prefer a church that had no strictness of doctrine, no sternness of rebuke, and no warnings of the wrath to come. Yet a Sabbath universally desecrated is worse than none. A Sabbath that sets loose the population of the land for recklessness, and riot, and drunkenness; a Sabbath without Sabbath instructions, Sabbath morals, and Sabbath religion; a Sabbath like the Sabbaths of Papal Europe, is such a day as must totally fail to secure any good end that belongs to the ordinance of God in Eden; and as must tend to demoralize rather than to bless society. Whether the opponents of our Sabbath laws see this end or not, the true tendency of Sabbath desecration is to strike a fatal blow at all the valuable influences, both physical

7*

and moral, that are exerted by the due observance of the sacred day.

But as the Sabbath has proved itself a day for perpetual observance by its continued recognition among all nations of Christendom, and even among those who retain it merely as a holiday, it becomes us to inquire, How ought it to be spent? As marriage remains every where upon earth, and yet from all its corrupted forms we must look back to Paradise to find its true law; so let the original and authoritative ordinations teach us the true law of the Sabbath. If it binds now, it binds for the same purposes and designs as ever. It still remains the Sabbath; and as it has its place, so it has its claims and character in the fourth commandment: while its just interpretation is to be found in all that is said of it in the word of God.

The Sabbath to Adam in Eden was a rest from the ordinary occupations of other days. And surely, since the fall of man and the more burdensome labour that pertains to our present estate, the claims of such a day are incomparably greater, as a needful rest from the severity of incessant toil. And the argument is complete which proves, from the physical necessities of man and beast, that such a day is needful for the health and life, as well as the comfort of God's creatures. If there is any difference between our own age and others, it may justly be affirmed that the rest of the Sabbath was never before so necessary as it is now, and shall always hereafter be, since the introduction of machinery to do the work of man. For the man whose daily labours require him to keep pace with the working of a steam engine, and to match his muscles with its untiring sinews, must toil with a watchfulness and a regularity hitherto unknown in all the labours of the race. And it is plain to every intelligent observer, that the energy and industry of our style of civilization must demand for the good of mind and body a cessation from these wearing toils, that is greatly more imperative than under any other form of human life. The truth is, we need this regular weekly rest more than man ever needed it before; and the prospect is, that as the race advances, man may look up with increasing thankfulness to God, for this institution of Paradise. Especially may toiling men thank God for the Sabbath. The poet is right with all his emphasis as he sings:

"Hail, Sabbath! thee I hail, the poor man's day!
For on this day, embosomed in his home,
He shares the frugal meal with those he loves;
With those he loves he shares the heartfelt joy
Of giving thanks to God—not thanks of form
A word and a grimace, but reverently,
With covered face and upward, earnest eye."*

In the happy land where we live, we hardly know what a poor man is; and descriptions of poverty in other lands are inapplicable here. Among us, dis

* Grahame.

tinctions of rank are unknown — distinctions of wealth are scarcely recognized. Health and energy have hitherto sufficed among us to secure a livelihood above a competence; and even in what we call "hard times," the miserable dependence and the unceasing toil of the poor in the crowded populations of Europe and Asia are unknown. Yet many things prove that things are even now changing in this respect. We have more poor than formerly; and the toil and energy necessary to secure a livelihood are greater than before; and there are more in our communities than there used to be, who secure employment with difficulty. And should things grow worse in this direction, should we ever have here the ceaseless struggle for life and bread that falls to the lot of the poor in eastern lands, we shall know, as we have never yet known, what it is for the poor to be in the power of the rich; and what a blessing God provided for the poor when in the garden of Eden he appointed the rest of the Sabbath. The Sabbath is needed, will be more and more needed in this toiling world. The busy population of these growing states are the last that, for their own sakes, dare trample upon it; and now is the time to fix the habits of this nation as a Sabbath-keeping people. Let the working men of America engage in such pleasure of Sabbath-desecration as must lay the burden of toil upon some of their own brethren, and ere long they will bring the curse of unceasing toil upon themselves. Let our working men consent to labour upon the Sabbath for any set of masters, and they not only make slaves of themselves, but they prepare heavier chains of bondage for their children, which, unless through the preventing mercy of a long suffering God, will weigh them down to the dust. Let the Sabbath of our fathers be given unimpaired to our children!

The truth is, the Sabbath and marriage are twin institutions; like Adam and Eve, both created in Eden, designed to live together, designed to support each other, and joined by God himself in bonds which no man should sunder. The toil of the week necessarily separates the husband from the wife, the parent from the child. If every day was a day of toil, some men would scarcely snatch an hour of domestic enjoyment; and the instruction of their children would seem scarcely a part of the duty devolving upon parents. The Sabbath is designed to further the ends not only of individual improvement, but of family benefit and comfort; and its hours are to be used accordingly. Nor is it any objection to this view, that so many disregard this influence of Sabbath hours. For we fearlessly challenge investigation when we allege, that no families are happier, or better trained, or more prosperous, than those in which the Sabbath is most carefully kept.

The Sabbath is most important in its influence upon the Family; and let men keep the Sabbath in such a way as to promote the advantage of all the families of man, and its other duties would scarcely be left undone. For if I must be with my family, then I ought not to keep my neighbour away from his; and if every family aimed to spend the Sabbath for the comfort and profit of the household, not only would all needless labour cease, but man would learn his great duties as a reasonable and an immortal creature. And it ought to be observed in support of these views that the fourth commandment is specially addressed to heads of families; and they are directed not only to keep holy the Sabbath, but to take care that it is so kept by all within their doors, whether children, or servants, or strangers. Richard Baxter is reported as saying, that when parents do their duty by their children, the conversion of souls will seldom take place in the sanctuary. The children will be brought to God while still under the parental roof. Happy day when every family shall be truly a nursery whence the plants of grace shall be brought to fill up the Church as the garden of the Lord. Give us a Sabbath in every family—as God gave the Sabbath and the family together in Paradise—and the morning star of that dawn will rise.

For the Sabbath is not only a day of rest. If we have it now in perpetuity, why should we not have it as it was in the beginning! When God gave a Sabbath, he sanctified it; when he repeated it in the moral law, he enjoined that it should be kept holy. The Sabbath is a religious day. As God gave it to Adam in his estate of innocence, this was its chief design. Rest from labour he needed less than man has ever needed it since; for the toil of a curse-stricken earth did not yet lay its burdens upon him. If any living man ever could refuse to sanctify a Sabbath because every day was holy, Adam might well say this; and yet in a life that knew no sin, he needed a day when his ordinary employments must be laid aside, and the whole time be spent in religious duties. And it is not a hard thing to understand that the physical rest which the sacred day now gives to the sons of toil, is not at all inconsistent with the design of this day, as holy to the service of God. A true rest for the mind and for the body is better secured, because these separated hours may not be spent in the active pursuit of folly and pleasure. No men appreciate or improve more the Sabbath, as a day of rest, than those who spend it most carefully as a religious day. Many spend these hours in seeking their own pleasure, which God's word expressly forbids; and they often show the result of this, by being more unfit for their usual duties upon Monday morning than at any other time in the week. Let the Sabbath be kept according to its own nature, and the design of its institution. God has blessed the day as one to be kept holy; and happy is the man who observes it accordingly.

There is scarcely any more important question to be settled in this land than that which pertains to the observance of the Sabbath in our communities.

It is impossible that the government of a free people can be maintained on this great continent, unless a substantial basis is laid in the intelligence and virtue of our citizens. And it is certainly true that the educational interests of this land have been chiefly promoted by Sabbath-loving and Sabbath-keeping men. And the Sabbath is the chief safeguard of virtue for this people. To its influence we owe all the difference that exists between us and the nations of Europe, who are now sending in upon our shores so many vices; and the cause of them all in an utter disavowal of the sanctity of the Sabbath. Break down the Sabbath, and all that is valuable in religion must be broken down with it. Only one nation of Europe ever ventured formally to blot the sacred day from existence; and the results are so horrible that the nations shut their ears at the dreadful cry, and trembled as they gazed. Yet before that reign of terror, France had only the semblance of a Sabbath. If even that could not be thrown off without such scenes of anarchy and bloodshed, as the just judgments of God upon a nation mad in infidelity, no mind can conceive the fearful consequences which would follow the downfall of such a Sabbath as these States have had since their settlement. Let every patriot, out of regard for the well being of his country, stand by the Sabbath. Every year proves that we need it more than ever, and just in proportion as its enemies become bold, and as Sabbath desecration increases, do we learn on every hand that crimes of every kind and grade are on the increase. The downfall of the Sabbath would be the Jubilee of evil.

As the Sabbath began in the earthly Eden, so it is a type of the heavenly Paradise. Heaven itself is called a Sabbatism—a rest that remaineth for the people of God. They who love and keep these hours of sacred time most cheerfully, keep in mind also the rest beyond.

> "Thine earthly Sabbaths, Lord, we love,
> But there's a nobler rest above;
> To that our longing souls aspire
> With ardent hope and strong desire."

Truly blessed are they who by the rest of God on earth are fitted to enter upon the songs and joys of that unending Sabbath.

Our great English poet has made us familiar with two important themes: Paradise Lost, and Paradise Regained. In the Paradise which our first father lost, God instituted the family and the Sabbath. When men are wise enough to keep both these ordinances according to their original appointment, they are ever found among the most efficient means through which, by Divine grace, we may regain the better Paradise.

CHAPTER IX.

THE ORIGIN OF EVIL.

"History not wanted yet,
Leaned on her elbow, watching Time, whose course,
Eventful, should supply her with a theme."

COWPER.

THE father of profane history informs us that he saw in Egypt an architectural wonder more surprising than the pyramids. This was their famous Labyrinth, built on the Lake Moeris; a magnificent pile of twelve palaces communicating with each other, having three thousand rooms, interspersed with terraces, half above ground and half below, having no apparent outlet. The rooms, and passages, and columns, were so numerous, and so similar to each other, that no stranger, once introduced, could find his way out without a guide. Hence, in common language, a labyrinth is a difficulty that cannot be explained, a confused mass of things hard to disentangle.

Virgil narrates that Dædalus, the architect of a similar labyrinth in Crete, taught Theseus how to find his way out, by unwinding a thread as he went in, and making it his guide upon his return.*

It would be a very easy thing for us to lose our way at this point of the history of our first father, in a more perplexing labyrinth than Greece or Egypt ever constructed. Here comes before us one of the most difficult and profound subjects of human thought; here indeed is a labyrinth where many have wandered, seeking in vain to find a solution. How did sin find entrance to the heart of a holy being? Rather, how could it find existence in the dominions of a holy, just, omniscient, and omnipotent God? This indeed is evidently not its first entrance. For the sin of man was through a tempter, who, before this, had sinned against the Creator. But how did sin find entrance into a holy world? is a question that naturally arises as we read of man's first disobedience.

Some boldly affirm that God is himself the Author of sin. They argue, that so vast is his knowledge, so unbounded his resources, so complete his power, that so entirely do creatures live, and move, and have their being in him, that the creature is nothing and God is everything. But this is certainly not the thread to lead us safely forth from these tangled mazes. We may agree with these persons in magnifying the supreme excellencies of Jehovah, but we are fully convinced, by reason of these very

* Æneid vi. 27. The true version is that Ariadne gave the clew.

perfections, that their conclusions cannot possibly be true. Whether we are or are not able to point out the sophistry, we know that reasonings, which reach such a conclusion, must be false. We have testimony, more direct and more complete, to convince us that this result is untrue, than is needful to overpower the force of any metaphysical reasonings in its favour. Every well regulated mind instantly rejects the thought as blasphemy, when told that God is the Author of sin. Every man's conscience accuses or excuses himself; gives him pleasure or grief in view of his own conduct and character; and seals the sentence of judgment against him as the author of his own sin. And the Scriptures say most explicitly, that God is most holy, cannot be tempted of evil, and tempts no man. Those who teach this blasphemy cannot guide us forth from the labyrinth.

As little are they correct guides, by whatever name they may call themselves, who affirm that sin is an evil to which a universe of rational beings is necessarily liable; that God himself is unable to prevent moral beings from sinning; that, having formed them free, it is beyond even *his* power to preserve them in holiness and happiness. This especial teaching has been very zealously supported in our own land, and at one time threatened to bring in the most serious evils upon our churches.

Dr. Taylor of New Haven, in a sermon preached at the commencement in Yale College in 1828, said,

"It is a groundless assumption that God could have prevented all sin, or at least, the present degree of sin in a moral system." So two years afterwards he wrote in the Christian Spectator, "Free moral agents can do wrong under all possible preventing influence," 1830, page 563. And afterwards, "We know that a moral system necessarily implies the existence of free agents, with the power to act in despite of all opposing power. This fact sets human reason at defiance, in every attempt to prove that some of these agents will not use that power and actually sin." 1831, page 617. So Prof. Charles G. Finney, at one time a revival-preacher in the Presbyterian Church, and afterwards professor of Theology at Oberlin, says, "It is vain to talk of God's omnipotence preventing sin." And similar teachings find expression elsewhere. Arminians teach that God did all he could to prevent sin, "consistently with his determination to give and maintain free agency to his creatures."* But we need not inquire further among whom these views are held. According to this theory, if God would make moral beings at all, he must, so to speak, run the risk of their sinning, a matter which he could not prevent. We may prefer to receive almost any other teaching upon this profound topic rather than believe this. Put this thread in our hands, and instead of guiding us upward and onward to the light of day, it leads us downward and inward to the darkest and gloomi-

* Watson's Institutes, P. ii. ch. xxviii.

est chambers beyond all hope. We regard it as destructive of some of the most distinctive and most precious teachings of the inspired volume; and as dishonouring God almost beyond conception. He is no longer a Sovereign; the creatures he has made are quite beyond his control; he may wish, and he may make all possible efforts, to effect his purposes; but men and devils will do as they please in spite of him. They are independent of him, and as a necessary consequence he is not independent of them. He may form his plans, but so far as they are concerned, his purposes may not be carried out. If these things are true, we cannot depend on the prophecies of the Bible; for men may refuse to do what God has said they will, and he has no power to produce the results predicted. We cannot trust its promises; we ought never to pray that God would advance any cause that depends on man's instrumentality.

The necessary consequences of these teachings are so dreadful that we shrink back from them with horror. "To be a free agent necessarily implies a liability to sin." We do not believe it. To be in a state of probation as Adam was, may imply this; but free agency does not. We believe that God can establish a free agent in holiness and happiness beyond the possibility of fall for ever. "If God," says Dr. E. D. Griffin, "could not have prevented sin in all worlds and ages, he cannot prevent sin in any world or age, or in any creature at any time, except by preventing the particular occasion and temptation. If God could not have prevented sin in the universe, he cannot prevent believers from fatally falling. He cannot prevent Gabriel and Paul from sinking at once into devils, and heaven from turning into a hell. And were he to create new races to fill the vacant seats, they might turn to devils as fast as he created them, in spite of any thing he could do, short of destroying their moral agency. He is liable to be defeated in all his designs, and to be as miserable as he is benevolent. This is infinitely the gloomiest idea that was ever thrown upon the world. It is gloomier than hell itself. For this involves only the destruction of a part; but that involves the wretchedness of God and his whole creation. And how awfully gloomy as it respects the prospects of individual believers! You have no security that you shall stand an hour. And even if you get to heaven, you have no certainty of remaining there a day."*

There is however another view of this matter which we seem bound to take. We do not pretend that the difficulties of the subject can be solved by us. But a thread may guide us through the labyrinth, if we do not understand the entire plan of its halls and passages. This thread is the simple principle, that, in religion as well as in natural philosophy, we are bound to recognize all the facts that are brought to our knowledge, even when we cannot

* Divine Efficiency, 180.

explain their connection, or even their consistency. All truths are consistent; but it is not a prerequisite to our knowledge of any truth that we are able to point out how it is consistent with other things. We believe that God is the full, necessary, and perpetual Sovereign of the universe; that at all times and in all things he doeth according to his pleasure in heaven and on earth; and yet that he so governs free creatures that their freedom is secured in the most perfect harmony with the execution of his great purposes. Though then he could have prevented the entrance of sin into the universe; and though we cannot determine the reasons why he did not, we believe he permitted it to enter. We know his supreme independence; his sovereign power; his ability to plan and to foretell the future, even in regard to those things which concern the free actions of even sinful beings. We know that sin exists; that sinners act freely; that their consciences condemn them for it; and that God holds them responsible. We know that his Spirit regenerates the hearts of sinful men, yet without interfering with their free agency; that believers in the gospel of Christ are surely "kept by the power of God through faith unto salvation," so that they cannot be separated from the love of Christ; and that the holy angels and the spirits of redeemed men in heaven are confirmed in holiness and happiness for ever beyond the possibility of fall, though they are as free moral agents as it is possible for creatures to be: we know in full consistency with all these facts that sin does exist, and that God will glorify himself in the great scheme of redemption from sin. Here we must stop. Why he has allowed sin to enter, we can only partially understand. But his sovereignty and man's freedom, his holiness and man's sin, are truths settled in our firm faith, beyond the reach of the most subtle sophistry and the most malignant cavils.

Yet while we may wisely decline all attempts to fathom the deep counsels of God in this great thing, there are two matters to which we may justly give our thoughts: First, we may vindicate the supremacy and the righteousness of God, as in the views just now expressed: and secondly, we may believe that God designs by the plan of salvation to show to the universe his wonderful wisdom, perhaps as it could not otherwise be shown. Eph. iii. 10. We do not know whether God's justice could be understood while his law was never broken; certainly his mercy could never be exercised without sinful objects; and above all, the harmony of justice and mercy in actual exercise, required a scheme like that of the gospel of Christ.

CHAPTER X.

THE GREAT TEMPTER.

> "For whence
> But from the author of all ill, could spring
> So deep a malice, to confound the race
> Of mankind in one root?"
>
> MILTON.

OUR attention, as we draw near the scene of temptation, is first called to the Tempter. He is here described as a serpent. Nor need we doubt that the animal spoken of was a kind of serpent; though one modern commentator has ventured to express a fantastic opinion on this point, and thus early in his commentaries upon the entire Bible, to bid us beware of trusting too much to such a judgment. If even we had any doubts of the true meaning of the Hebrew word here translated as serpent, the point would be settled by the authority of the New Testament. For there it is declared that the serpent beguiled Eve; and we need have no doubts of the true meaning of the Greek word there used. It may possibly be that the whole tribe of serpents was originally formed to move in a more erect posture than they now do; as we know that now some species of serpents, especially when excited, are accustomed to move with their heads considerably elevated from the ground.

But temptation almost always comes in insidious and deceitful forms; its plausible pretensions give it its chief currency; and we must be upon our guard against things that seem harmless. The serpent was an animal endowed with subtlety above the other creatures; yet the serpent was but an instrument. The true tempter was another, an intelligent being, making use of this form to serve his wicked purpose of deceiving man and of leading him to sin. The Scriptures reveal the tempter under the name of Satan—an adversary. The Apostle John not only tells us that the devil sinneth from the beginning; but he gives him the various names of the dragon, that old serpent, and Satan. Who this adversary was and is, we are also informed. Sin did not begin in the universe with the family of man. There are angels whom God created in holiness and happiness, who kept not their first estate, and who were cast down from heaven and are now reserved in chains of darkness until the judgment of the great day. The chief of these is called the devil, Beelzebub, Apollyon, and Satan. Men have indeed professed to doubt the existence of this adversary, and of such powerful adversaries to man as the fallen angels. Yet while we can easily decide that the designs of such an adversary can be all the more busily and successfully carried forward, if he can add this to his other deceits that men should be persuaded that he has no existence; we may as easily see the proofs of what he is and what he can do, in the sad history of the world, behind us and around us. But we need have no doubts upon this subject, if we receive in simple confidence the clear and explicit statements of the Bible.

This sacred volume reveals to us a world of spiritual beings, having much intercourse with men, of whom we would be ignorant but for its teachings.

> "Millions of spiritual creatures walk the earth
> Unseen, both when we wake and when we sleep."

Why God permits the fallen angels to exert their powers of evil and to tempt man—like a vast chamber in the great labyrinth to whose high roof and distant walls our eyes, at least in these abodes of darkness, cannot see—is a branch of the great question concerning the origin of evil which we cannot understand. The simple and serious facts we may well know—Satan is a powerful, wicked, malignant foe of man. He is, in the sacred writings, represented as the god of this world, the prince of the power of the air, and the accuser of God's people, who accuses them night and day before God. 2 Cor. iv. 4. Eph. ii. 2. Rev. xii. 10. He works in the children of disobedience. Eph. ii. 2; blinds the eyes of them that believe not, 2 Cor.

iv. 4; leads captive wretched souls at his will, 2 Tim. ii. 26; and catches away the truth from the hearts of those that hear the gospel, lest they should believe and be saved, Luke viii. 12. So great is his presumption that he did not forbear to assault the Son of God himself when he became incarnate, and attempt to beguile him by subtlety. Of such an adversary; of his subtle deceits; and of the means of our safety, it is our folly to be ignorant. For no believer on earth is safe from his attacks. And this is a matter well worthy of our frequent and serious study—to know the arts of this great Tempter. From the first scene in Paradise to the present time, he has prosecuted his plans to lead men away from God. He transforms himself into an angel of light; he misrepresents both the truth to make it appear burdensome, and the falsehood to make it seem attractive; he is a liar and a murderer from the beginning, not to be trusted in any word he says, and to be feared in all he aims to do.

CHAPTER XI.

MAN'S FIRST SIN.

"Her rash hand in evil hour
Forth reaching to the fruit, she plucked, she ate;
Earth felt the wound, and nature from her seat
Sighing through all her works gave signs of woe
That all was lost."

MILTON.

THE first sin of man has been thought, by some, an insignificant act to be followed by consequences so serious. It is a difficult task to weigh accurately the actions of men. But we can easily decide that the deeds of men are not to be estimated by the magnitude of individual acts, by the time occupied in doing them, or even by their consequences; but rather by the principles involved in them, and the motives of the actors. The sin of our first parents was a serious offence, not only as the first sin of man, but because it was attended by many circumstances which a righteous judgment would regard as aggravations of their iniquity.

They had no apology for desiring the fruit of this tree. The wise man says, "Men do not despise a thief if he steal to satisfy his soul when he is hungry." Prov. vi. 30. That is, when a man must starve or eat what is not his own, necessity affords some extenuation for appropriating the goods of another. But God had filled that fruitful garden with every good and beautiful tree, to which this first pair had free access; they were the rich possessors of abundance, more than they could use; and they should have cast no longing eyes towards that single tree which alone had been forbidden.

The singleness of the tree, the simplicity of the Divine command, and the confession of the parties, prove that they erred through no misapprehension of the right. There are complicated moral questions which perplex even sincere inquirers after truth; and error seems less flagrant when adopted ignorantly. But the first sin was not such a case. Adam and Eve knew very well the command laid upon them. No deep argument, or long reflection, or practical experience was necessary to teach them what they should do. The direction was so plain that a child could not misunderstand; nor did they ever allege, even in their guilt, that they had not fully known their duty.

The happy pair in Eden were under the greatest possible obligation to obey the God who commanded them not to eat of that tree. They knew him; knew his holy character; knew what blessings he had already bestowed upon them; and their Maker and Benefactor had claims which should have kept them steadfast in their obedience. Their offence was worse that they listened to the voice of such a tempter. It may be that they thought not of Satan; perhaps they knew nothing of him; they saw here possibly only a serpent; but no living creature should have borne comparison in their minds with their glorious God; and they should not have believed the words of any creature—insignificant or otherwise—in preference to the words of their Creator.

Moreover, our first parents were distinctly forewarned that death would result from eating of this fruit. The full meaning of the term and the fearful things included in it, they may not have understood. Doubtless the earth would have known many changes by death and like death, if man had never sinned. The seasons would have gone their rounds and brought their necessary mutations. If spring brought forth its blades and blossoms, every seed must die before the shoot appeared; every flower must fall before the fruit could form or ripen; and autumn, then as now, must have been a season of seared and fallen leaves. So the beasts of the earth would die in their times. But during man's brief estate of innocency he may have seen too little even of these things, to give him any deep impressions of the meaning of the term, death. Adam may have had a low and feeble idea of the evil thus threatened. But sinners very seldom do form either a just or a definite idea of the result of their sins. Perhaps no transgressor ever fully anticipated the end of his transgression. It is not needful to the most complete responsibility that the mind should know all the results of our conduct. It is enough if the law is fairly known and the liability of the sinner to a righteous penalty is recognized. Our first parents knew that to eat of that fruit would bring upon them the disapproval and displeasure of the God who had forbidden it. And the Divine displeasure—if continued—would itself imply the most serious meaning of this term, death, even when it refers to an immortal being. Surely no soul can be happy when God is displeased. The wretchedness of the sinner—especially of one, who, like Adam, had known God's favour—must result from his separation from God.

In contrast with the threatened penalty, was the promise fairly implied. Even supposing that our first father understood the promise as little as he did the threatening; that is, that he was equally unable fully to anticipate the blessings of life eternal, and the dread meaning of death eternal; yet he knew clearly that by his obedience he would retain the highest source of permanent happiness in the favour and approbation of God. No inducement should have prevailed to lead him to such an exchange of God's approbation for his displeasure.

Nor should we forget another consideration of the very gravest kind, which should have kept back our first parents from that great offence. The first man, Adam, stood not for himself alone, but as the head and representative of all his unborn children. We have no detailed and formal account in these early chapters of Genesis, of the covenant so made with Adam as to make him the representative of the human family. Many therefore have denied that he did sustain any such relation. Yet all who properly consider this important matter ought to acknowledge these two things:

First, Adam stood towards the entire human family exactly in that relation which will harmonize all the teachings that God has given us in regard to him. We are bound to hear, not only the book of Genesis, but all the word of God: nor should we fail to gather rays of light from the teachings of his providence. Upon this matter David, and Hosea, and Paul are witnesses as competent as Moses; and we must receive all the later expositions of the Bible which throw light upon the earlier narratives.

Second, the real relation held towards the race by Adam was doubtless understood by him. We are not to measure his knowledge by the brief records of his times; it is no violent presumption to suppose that he knew the truth upon a point of such importance, even though we are left to gather the entire truth from far later teachings.

Let us keep these thoughts in view. The personal duty of Adam to obey God would be the same, whether we consider him as acting simply under a law, or as acting under a covenant. His responsibility in transgression is greatly increased, if he knew that he acted in a public capacity—as the head and representative of the human race: and in this we may find a strong reason for believing that the true state of the case was not unknown to him. But we say these things not as undervaluing the teachings of Genesis. We think that we can gather proofs from the brief narrative that our first father had a full understanding of all that is implied in a covenant, and gave his full consent to all its terms.

1. Man was bound to perfect obedience. Of this the fruit of the forbidden tree was made a special test; and man accepted of the test. So Eve declared, We may eat of every tree but this.

2. Death was the threatened penalty of disobedience.

3. Life was promised upon his obedience. This is fairly implied; and the subsequent Scriptures often assert it. "Moses describeth the righteousness which is of the law, that the man which doeth these things shall live by them." Rom. x. 5.

4. Not only Adam but all his children after him were included in this covenant. The proof of this begins with Eve's recognition of the covenant as binding her, though made with Adam; it is strengthened by the actual sentence pronounced, by its execution in succeeding ages, and by the teachings of

the subsequent Scriptures which we may notice hereafter.

Surely if Adam understood that this was his relation to our race, his sin was one of great enormity. And different from the opinion often held upon this matter, we may not forget to add that the very insignificance of the act in itself considered, is a remarkable aggravation of that first offence. When very strong inducements are held out to lead any one from the path of virtue, we feel more pity for the transgressor than when one exchanges innocence for guilt upon trifling grounds. We honour a defeated commander who bravely holds his post as long as possible against superior forces; we reproach the cowardice of one who surrenders at the first call, without a struggle, and to a feebler force. It makes the matter worse, not better, that Adam sold Eden, innocence, life, and God's favour for the forbidden fruit.

For reasons like these we cannot agree with the opinions of those who make light of man's first sin, or who think that matters too grave were made to depend upon too small a thing. The smaller the inducement to transgression, the greater the advantage to man in innocence. The excellent plenty of all the garden, contrasted with the fruit of a single tree and the slight gratification it could afford; the simplicity of the command which precluded all possibility of mistake; the obligations under which he was to God, and the folly of believing any creature who spoke in plain contradiction of the Creator; the penalty and the promise; the knowledge that interests so great were involved in that solemn covenant; and the very insignificance of that tempting fruit; all these things make the transgression of Adam most serious indeed. And finally his first estate; no bias of sin inclining him to evil, no darkness of understanding clouding his views, in perfect holiness, having everything to make him happy, must be thought the aggravation of his offence. His inexperience of evil was an advantage. For he was advertised of his danger; the very name of the forbidden tree was a warning; and innocence is a better protection against threatening evils, than a partial experience has ever proved to be. We rank Adam among the chief of sinners, and esteem the first sin as one of peculiar enormity. Applying our usual tests to ascertain the heinous nature of any offence, we can have no sympathy with those who judge man's first offence a trifle.

CHAPTER XII.

THE TEMPTATION.

WE may now draw near the scene of temptation. We have no just reason to think that the inspired records give us a full account of any part of the history. These are brief sketches, not full details. The words of Moses have been compared to our modern telegraphic despatches; few words are used to express a great deal of meaning; we learn much, yet we crave more, especially in regard to these important early scenes, we greatly desire fuller communications. "Who is there among us that would not give twenty of the best volumes from his shelves, for twenty lines which should acquaint him with the condition of our first parents during the first years after the fall and their expulsion from paradise?"* And truly a larger knowledge of the fall itself would be no less interesting.

The tempter, we are told, approached not Adam, but Eve, apparently by herself and unguarded. The Apostle Paul says that "Adam was not de-

* Kitto Bible Ill.

ceived, but the woman being deceived was in the transgression." 1 Tim. ii. 14. Some understand this to mean that Adam, finding that Eve had already transgressed, chose to join her, though fully aware of the evil consequences. This is the interpretation put upon his first sin by Milton in Paradise Lost. But the apostle may simply mean that Eve sinned first.

Notice the manner of his approach, that we may learn his methods in temptation. He begins by insinuating, rather than by expressing, hard thoughts of God. He affects to feel surprise that any tree of the garden should be forbidden to them. But having engaged her attention and awakened a train of reflections suitable for his purposes, he speaks plainly and boldly in contradiction of the kindness of their Creator. And we may well notice that deceivers often command our belief of the barest and most mischievous falsehoods, by the very boldness and assurance with which they assert them. Our confidence is naturally called forth towards sincerity, and error often spreads because its bold advocates seem sincere. Satan is first surprised that God had forbidden this tree; but how soon he ventures to deny boldly that the prohibition is disinterested! He declares that death shall not follow their eating of it, and that, indeed, knowledge like to God himself will result. Nor is it unlikely that he appealed to the very name of the tree as a confession, that a desirable knowledge beyond their present estate, would be secured by their eating.

Doubtless advantage was taken to address our first mother when she stood in sight of the tree itself. "The woman saw that the tree was good for food." There is danger in drawing near temptation, even when we are aware of its nature, and are most upon our guard. The wise man warns us, "Avoid it, pass not by it, turn from it, and pass away." The voice of the tempter finds a great auxiliary in the eye of the tempted; alas! we are already in greater peril when we consent to look. Eve heard a voice at which she should have stopped her ear the moment she understood the object; she looked upon that fair fruit just when she ought to have turned away.

We may not be able to trace the course of feeling in the first transgressor. But distrust of God seems to have been the first wrong thought. And when jealousy of him entered her mind, "when Eve let go her hold upon that glorious benefactor, till then absolutely loved, venerated, and trusted, she was prepared for every thing which could follow."* She could begin then to believe that the advantages promised by the tempter should indeed be hers. And when in obedience already to a false lord, she looked upon the tree; when the lust of the eye made way for the lust of the flesh, the pride of being like God was not far off. The tree was pleas-

* Dwight's Theology, i. 407.

ant to the sight; here is the lust of the eye. It was good for food; here is the appetite for sensual indulgence. It was a tree to be desired to make one wise; here is the pride of life.

This sin, like so many that have succeeded it in human experience, came into gradual strength to secure her downfall. She indulged irreverent thoughts of God: she desired to taste the beautiful fruit; she aspired to the expected knowledge, that she might be as God; she hoped that the threatened evil would not result. In all this scene, though the matter is of so great importance, Eve seems to have relied wholly upon her own strength. We hear of no counselling with Adam, though they were mutual helpers, and he doubtless was not far off. We hear of no looking up to God in this hour of need. How many prayers, how many agonizing petitions for the pardon of sin, would have been spared by one brief petition then offered for sin's prevention!

She looked upon the tree, desired it, partook of it. Nor was this all. Then she sought for her husband, and turning tempter in her turn, as sinners usually do, she gave also to her husband, and he did eat. Thus sin entered our world. "Behold how great a matter a little fire kindleth." This is the beginning; who can tell the end? Well might our great English poet represent the sympathy of suffering nature in this sad event.

"Earth trembled from her entrails . . . .
Nature gave a groan,
Sky lowered and muttering thunder some sad drops
Wept at completing of the mortal sin
Original."

PAR. LOST, ix.

Among the immediate consequences of this sin upon our first parents, we may notice that they did indeed gain a knowledge of good and evil; but in no such sense as they understood from the words of the tempter. They felt immediately shame at their own nakedness, and attempted by a frail covering of fig leaves to clothe themselves. But they felt also, now for the first time, unwilling to meet the God whose displeasure they knew they deserved. And see here not only the fears but the usual deceits of sin. They are foolish enough to attempt concealment even from the eye of God. And when their hiding among the trees of the garden so little availed them, we find that these unhappy sinners have learned the language of falsehood. But even their untrue reason for concealing themselves only serves for an undesigned confession of their guilt. And when the searching inquiry is made if they had eaten of the tree, we see the usual characteristic of sin in the self-justifying spirit that would throw the blame any where else but upon themselves.

Our first parents show in this first interview with their Maker, not only that they are sinners, but impenitent sinners. They are ashamed; they are conscience stricken; but they use concealment, falsehood, and self justification. We are not to regard them as hardened offenders; but neither are they humble and penitent. Indeed they had no just ground for approaching their offended God with any hope of acceptance; and we do not believe that true penitence toward him has ever existed in any guilty mind, save as it is awakened in view of his readiness to forgive. The prospects before the mind of fallen Adam were dark indeed. Foolish as he was to hide from God, it was quite natural that he should shrink from seeing Him; and yet, alas! the tree has added very little to his stock of knowledge, if he judges that his falsehoods can pass undiscovered.

See in them the proof that it is not in the power of outward things to bestow happiness upon the soul of man. Adam and his wife were still in that happy Paradise which God had specially prepared for their comfort. The same cool walks invited them; the same shady trees protected them; the same ripe fruits hung around to invite their taste; and they still had each other's society. But the garden was not the same to them. A new crowd of thoughts within changed all the aspects of nature without. Fear, suspicion, shame, and guilt are the new inhabitants of Eden; and peace, and happiness, and even hope fled as these took possession of the noblest dwelling place in the garden—the only palace God had built in Paradise—even the heart of man.

And here we may see that, had man been left to himself, the breach between him and God would have been irreparable. He no longer desires to see God; he hides himself from his presence. He is not a hardened sinner, but already he feels like shunning God. And if this was his state of mind, it is not the natural tendency of sin to make things any better. If Adam had voluntarily come before God frankly confessing his offence, it would seem ingenuous and right. He had committed but one sin; he had formerly known God's favour; his heart was not made obdurate by repeated offences. Yet he made no movement of this kind. And as we know that these matters always grow worse rather than better; as repeated sin hardens the heart and never softens it; as it sends men further and further away from God, and never seems to draw them closer; so we may reasonably believe that if Adam did not repent immediately upon the shame of his first offence, there was no natural tendency towards repentance in any future period of his course. The estrangement of man from God was total; every new step was further departure; death had already begun its work in him; and so long as Adam lived—if even he lived for ever—he could not look up with the filial feelings of a son towards

God, as his heavenly Father. There was no hope for man in that dreadful day; there was no hope for ever; unless God, by a mercy never before shown, should make the first overtures to heal the fearful breach.

CHAPTER XIII.

THE GOSPEL ANNOUNCED.

"Never was sung a sweeter word,
Nor fuller music e'er was heard,
Nor deeper aught the heart hath stirred."

How wretched, indeed, would the lot of our first parents have been, if God had dealt with them according to their sin; or waited to show mercy until they had first shown relentings and repentance! But having led them to an unwilling confession, before proceeding to pass upon them the sentence of his law, he judges their tempter and opens for them a door of hope. It may be true that many presumptuous men sin yet more because of the mercy of God; it is also true that a knowledge of his mercy is an essential element of evangelical repentance. Had God spoken his sentence first upon our first parents, despair must have filled their minds; but he intimates the plan of the gospel, before he declares the results of their sin, or sends them forth from Paradise.

The first sentence of the Divine displeasure is

pronounced upon the serpent. This may be considered in two parts:

First, there is the curse directed against the animal, the serpent itself. Satan had used this as an instrument to effect his evil purpose; and God so abhors sin, that the very instruments of it, fall under his curse. The serpent must go upon its belly and eat the dust; and its head must be bruised. Possibly, as we have before suggested, this animal previously moved in a spiral manner; now it must be prone. And the curse of enmity between it and man, exists yet to a remarkable degree. No class of animals is more universally dreaded and hated by man than the race of serpents. Nor can this fear and aversion spring from the venomous character of the reptile. Out of three hundred species of serpents in the world, two hundred and fifty are harmless; some of them are beautiful; all are graceful; and yet, by a kind of instinctive antipathy, men hate the sight of them. It is not even pleasant to talk about them. Even those that are known to be harmless are almost invariably killed as soon as seen; and the usual mode of killing a serpent is to break its head. These things wonderfully agree with this earliest prediction of the Bible.

Secondly, the burden of the curse did not rest upon the animal. The true tempter was Satan, and the curse is therefore chiefly upon him. But the sentence against man's malignant enemy is a blessing really upon the man. When, therefore, God declares that enmity shall exist between the woman and the serpent, between their seed respectively, and a conflict ending in the bruising of his head, he speaks a blessing to us. If our first parents had been in a suitable frame of mind, perhaps this blessing would have been addressed directly to them;* but as Adam has made only unwilling acknowledgments, God's designs of grace are revealed in the form of threatening against the serpent.

It is agreed among evangelical commentators that this sentence against Satan contains the first promise of the gospel. This is the germ—like a grain of mustard seed—from which springs forth that great tree beneath whose shade innumerable multitudes find rest and life.

It is not needful for us to ask, How much did our first parents understand of these words? It is rather our place to inquire, What do they really mean? Truth is like light; a very little of it is of invaluable excellence, though the clearer it is the better. Doubtless they knew more of the meaning of these words afterwards; but our understanding of truth does not always depend upon the clearness with which it is spoken. These expressive words imply plainly a conflict, especially between the seed of the woman and the seed of the serpent, in which the victory shall remain with the woman. This

* A. Fuller.

much our first parents might know as soon as they heard the voice of God; but we, who have seen this seed of Scriptural prophecies grow into larger predictions, and bring forth the fruit of actual fulfilment, may better know its fulness of meaning.

1. By the seed of the woman we may chiefly understand the great Redeemer our Lord Jesus Christ.

There are many reasons why the Saviour of fallen man should himself be a man. That in the same nature that had broken the law, obedience should be rendered and satisfaction made, seemed eminently proper. But to give us also boldness of access to God; and to enable him to sympathize with us, having a fellow-feeling of our infirmities, (Heb. ii. iii.); and in the superaboundings of God's grace, to advance the dignity of our nature, are the further Divine purposes in giving us a human Redeemer. But the Redeemer must not be only a man. A man and nothing more—a member of the fallen race in all its liabilities, could be no Saviour of the fallen. We may therefore expect to find, in this early proclamation of the gospel, a mystery; an enigmatical expression of truth to be explained hereafter. This bruiser of Satan's head is to be human, yet separated from the ordinary humanity; a man, yet not simply of the race; partaker of the nature, yet not partaker of the liabilities of the nature of man. Mark the expression, "the woman's seed." Mark the fact that, as man had already fallen, this promised Deliverer was not represented by Adam in the covenant of Eden. Not the seed of Adam, but of the woman; not promised before, but after the fall, there is but one person of all history who fully answers the terms of this first prophecy; the child born of a virgin in Bethlehem of Judea.

An interesting chapter of human opinions could easily be gathered in the illustrations which paganism affords of this first declaration of the gospel. The serpent plays a most important part in the fall of man, according to the traditions of many pagan nations. Dr. Kitto mentions an ancient bas-relief thus described:—"At one hand are a man and woman standing naked under a tree, the woman in a drooping and disconsolate posture, the man with one hand raised to the tree, and the other directed towards the woman. It is such a picture that a child would at once say, 'That is Adam and Eve.' At the other extremity is a sedate and august figure seated upon a rock and strangling the serpent with his hand."* "By consulting Moore's Hindu Pantheon it will be seen that the serpent, Caliya, is represented as the decided enemy of the mediatorial God, Krishna, whom he persecutes, and on whom he inflicts various sufferings, though he is at length vanquished. Krishna, pressed within the folds of the serpent, and then triumphing over him and bruising his head beneath his feet, is the subject of a very ancient Hindu bas-relief and carries with it

* Kitto, Bib. Ill. i. 60. Creuzer's Symbolik., pl. 158.

its own interpretation.*" So the great prince promised in the famous Sybilline leaves of the Romans, was to abolish injustice and violent death, kill the serpent, purge the earth of poisons, and establish universal peace.† But we need not add to these here. They seem evidently to spring from the remembrance of this first prophecy, as handed down through the channel of oral tradition.

2. But while the term, "the seed of the woman" applies primarily to none so well as to the Lord Jesus Christ—who was the son of the woman, and who was not a partaker of Adâm's fall—yet it is proper to understand it also of all the servants and followers of Christ. When Paul explains—Gal. iii. 16,—that the seed promised to Abraham preëminently signifies Christ, this does not prevent him from saying further that every believer in Christ is also of the seed of Abraham. Gal. iii. 26, 29. A man may be of the seed of Abraham naturally by his descent from Abraham: or he may be of his seed spiritually by being partaker of his principles, especially of his faith. The seed of the woman and the seed of the serpent do not merely signify the principal persons here named; the followers of Christ and the followers of Satan are also meant. So the Scriptures frequently teach that wicked men are the children of the devil. "Ye are of your father, the devil, and the lusts of your father ye will do," said our Lord to the Jews. John viii. 44.

* Watson's Theology, p. 20. † Virgil Buc. Ec. iv.

The children of God and the children of the devil are manifest by their principles and their works. 1 John iii. 10. In this just threatening against the tempter, the line of distinction is drawn to run through all time, to divide "between him that serveth God and him that serveth him not." Mal. iii. 18.

3. The words of this threatening imply a long struggle between conflicting parties, and the partial power of the wicked one to injure the woman's seed. The serpent was to bruise the heel of the seed of the woman.

The fierce warfare of wrong against right, of error against truth, of evil against good, is here foretold. Herein are signified the humiliation, sorrows, and death of the great Redeemer. Satan had the power to assault the Mediator; to raise up against him cruel and bloody men, and to put him to a shameful death. But his severest assaults were vain, and the sorest success did no permanent injury to the Sufferer. The prince of darkness had nothing in him. Even when he took his life, the cross was the scene of triumph, and the grave could not hold the victim. The heel is not a vital part; and all that Satan could effect against the incarnate Son of God was to as little purpose as if a man should bruise the heel of his adversary with a stone.

And herein is predicted that long conflict which has ever since existed between God's believing people and their great adversary. From the beginning there has been warfare. Cain slew Abel his brother, "because his own works were evil and his brother's righteous." 1 John iii. 12. And the fierceness of this strife has filled the world with grief. It is true indeed that shame, and strife, and violence, and wrong, fill even those portions of the earth where the sway of the god of this world is least disputed. But Satan fights hardest when the seed of the woman withstands him. The history of the church of God is full of the records of this most deadly strife. So a leader in the sacramental host exhorts us, "Beloved, think it not strange concerning the fiery trial that is to try you." 1 Pet. iv. 12. What an arsenal of weapons is at the command of Satan, and what a catalogue could the church furnish of the arms that have been used against her—lies, heresies, vain philosophy, subtle errors, earthly affections, love, fear, ambition, avarice, envy, and revenge. Those that would serve him have been drawn to him by gold, and lust, and power: those that dare oppose him have been the subjects of manifold persecutions. They have been reviled by the wise, scorned by the world, cast off by near and dear friends, and defamed shamefully in their most innocent doings. They have been stoned, sawn asunder, destitute, afflicted, banished to deserts, and mountains, and dens and caves; they have been cast to the wild beasts, beheaded, crucified; they have been racked with unheard of tortures, burned at the stake, and dishonoured in deeds without name; secluded in the dungeons of the Inquisition; exposed in the shame of an Auto da Fe; in short, crucified by pagans, burned by heretics, drowned by atheists, and massacred by every form of the serpent's seed. The time would fail to name the means; the time would fail to mention the numbers of those whom Satan has slain for the word of God and the testimony of Jesus.

Look back upon the history of the church in the light of human reason, and we may fear to enlist under her banners. What an array of sorrows and sufferings belongs here! Yet all these are sorrows for righteousness' sake; and the world's best blessings have been bought with the struggles and the blood of the people of Christ. But look on these things in the light of faith, and how different it seems! All these sorrows are but the bruising of a man's heel. Magnify them if you choose, and as much as you please; and so long as the promises of a faithful God declare that even in this life "we shall receive a hundred fold more;" that "the sufferings of this present time are not worthy to be compared with the glory that shall be revealed;" and that "our light affliction which is but for a moment worketh for us a far more exceeding and eternal weight of glory," we surely need not repine. If the bruising of the heel means so much and yet effects so little, the bruising of the serpent's head must be his utter destruction. But the end is not yet. Happy are they who endure the cross in patient waiting for the triumph.

It is our happiness to hear the gospel preached far more plainly than in its first intimation in dishonoured Eden. Let it not be our greater folly and guilt to neglect so great salvation.

CHAPTER XIV.

THE SENTENCE UPON EVE.

"Not she, with treacherous kiss, the Saviour stung,
Not she denied him with blaspheming tongue;
She, when apostles shrank, could danger brave,
Last at his cross and earliest at his grave."

WE have seen that the curse pronounced upon the tempter included in it a large blessing for sinful man. And we should not fail to admire the mercy of God which is thus declared to man, not only in advance of the sentence upon his guilt, but before any tokens of his repentance. We may now further see that even the sentence of condemnation, like a dark cloud, whose bright edges give notice that there is light behind, is mingled with tokens of Divine forbearance.

The sentence pronounced upon the woman is simple and easily understood; and the proof is full and abundant that it applies not to Eve alone, but to the entire succession of her daughters in all ages since. Attachment to her husband, subjection to his authority, and sorrow in the birth of her children, are elements in the common lot of woman. But there is just reason for declaring that good often springs forth from these very evils, and the sorrows of their estate have often proved a rich blessing to the female sex.

It is a very common remark that women are more religious than men. In our congregations, it is a very rare case where the attendance of women is not larger than that of men; more women make a profession of piety; fewer women disgrace their profession or decline from it; and, upon the average, their piety is more serious and deeper. The female sex have greatly the advantage in religious things, if we judge from the actual facts in Christian churches. And in systems of false religion, Satan, their author, seems to have an especial spite against the women. Made aware that his cunning in tempting the first woman is to recoil in special destruction upon his own head; knowing that woman is ever to effect much against him; and not ignorant, that if, as at the first, he can cast her down to sin, he can thus best war against the man, Satan has carried on his warfare most resolutely against the daughters of Eve, and wherever he rules, woman is sure to be degraded. It is, doubtless, also through his special enmity against woman, that among the heathen the unnatural but prevalent crime of infanticide is practised almost exclusively against their female children. We need not repeat what was said in a former chapter of the tendency of the Bible to speak kindly of woman, to elevate her condition, and to bless the entire race of man through her elevation.

The very sorrows of woman have been made subservient to her spiritual interests, wherever the Bible is known and she is instructed in its great teachings. She suffers more than man usually does; and the very quietness and seclusion of her ordinary duties tend to make her sufferings of a more profitable character. The very independence which man usually asserts is a great disadvantage; since true piety consists not in the exercise of pride, but specially in humility, meekness, forbearance, and patience. The trials which fall to the lot of woman are eminently adapted to call forth all these meeker emotions; she has less opportunity to shake off from her the influence of her cares. When men are vexed and troubled, they go forth to active duties in a busy, bustling world, and their griefs are lost in their cares for other things. It is quite otherwise with woman. When about her ordinary duties, she can let her mind dwell upon serious or afflicting thoughts; the quiet of home serves to make her impressions deeper; and if it sometimes happens that she lets her troubles prey too much upon her, because she has less opportunities to throw them off, or to unbosom them to others, yet she is frequently driven to tell her griefs at the throne of grace—the sanctuary for the afflicted, whose gates are not shut either by day or by night—and those sorrows are made happy which bring her to know the tender mercy of God. Let not the daughters of Eve repine. Through sorrow many a suffering woman has been led to him who dries the mourner's tears. Through sorrow many such have found the path to heaven. And many a sweet voice in the heavenly choirs will sing eternal praises for earth's bitter hours. And the bitterer earth is, the sweeter the song in heaven will be.

Through these sorrows, sanctified in woman's experience, God brings a blessing upon the race. For the sake of the entire family of man are these strong providential guards thrown around female piety. Children are usually what their mothers make them. The substantial character of most men is formed in early life; and in the most important period of existence, the influence of the mother is paramount. The cares and duties of the father—whatever may be his inclination—keep him away from his children. But the mother's chief cares are with them; they are almost constantly in her presence; their first lisping words they catch from her fond lips; they are scholars of hers from the very earliest age; they watch every expression of her eye; imitate her in every movement; and interpret and adopt her spirit. God has taken care that there shall be more piety among women, because he thus secures a more careful education of children in pious lessons. Children have before them the best and not the worst specimens of the race for their example. Even mothers who are not themselves pious, teach religious lessons to their children; restrain them from evil; wish them to fear God; and often are led themselves to Christ by responsibilities and anxieties which their children awaken. Few are the men who do not hold sacred and dear the memory of their mothers.

> "My mother's voice! How often creeps
> Its cadence o'er my lonely hours,
> Like healing sent on wings of sleep
> Or dew to the unconscious flowers;
> I can't forget her melting prayer
> E'en while my pulses madly fly,
> And in the still, unbroken air
> Her gentle tones come stealing by;
> And years, and sin, and manhood flee,
> And leave me at my mother's knee."

Surely this much may be added to these reflections: that piety is the crowning virtue of female character; that no woman can live in a land purified by the influence of Christianity, and can make the contrast between her condition and that of her unhappy sisters in foreign lands, and yet keep back her heart from the great Redeemer here revealed, without incurring guilt of a fearful and peculiar character. The Bible—woman's benefactor—should be every woman's blessed instructer. Jesus Christ, born of a woman, should be every woman's chosen Saviour. But especially, how unbecoming are scornful and scoffing words against religion upon woman's lips! There are some who ridicule religion; ridicule the seriousness of their companions; ridicule the truths and the ordinances of God; and speak jestingly of salvation and of the things that pertain to it. But those who descend to such guilt and folly certainly gain nothing to themselves of good or of honour. Especially no well taught, sensible man can ever be pleased with scoffs upon female lips. The very men who might join in such scorning, in the company of reckless men, turn with disgust from the cant of infidelity or the heartlessness of irreligion in a woman. The woman who can speak flippantly of marriage or of the Bible, strikes from beneath her own feet the bridge that bears her above a yawning chasm. So even the worldly poet before quoted expresses a just view of such a case.

"Oh, what is woman, what her smile,
Her look of love, her eyes of light,
What is she, if her lips revile
The lowly Jesus? Love may write
His name upon her marble brow,
And linger in her curls of jet;
The pale spring flowers may scarcely bow
Beneath her step; and yet, and yet
Without that meeker grace shall be,
A lighter thing than vanity!"

CHAPTER XV.

LABOUR.

"Oh mortal man who livest here by toil,
Do not complain of this thy hard estate;
That like an emmet thou must ever moil,
Is a sad sentence of an ancient date:
And, certes, there is reason for it great;
For though sometimes it makes thee weep and wail,
And curse thy day and early drudge and late,
Withouten that would come a heavier bale,
Loose life, unruly passions, and diseases pale."

THOMSON.

WE next consider some of the facts connected with the curse pronounced upon Adam.

The Lord God declared a curse upon the ground for man's sake. As the earth was created for man, as he is the only intelligent, rational, and immortal being upon it, so the globe is specially adapted to him, both in what it has, and in what it lacks; both in its blessings and in its curses. In the later Scriptures an apostle assures us that through man's sin the whole world groaneth, and the created things around us are made subject to vanity.

Yet as labour is necessary to the happiness of man, as it existed before the fall, and as it is only upon man, the sinner, that God laid it as a toilsome burden; we may believe that the curse spoken against the ground, consisted in using for the Divine purposes things which already existed, but that were not grievous until man had fallen under God's displeasure. We need not think that while man was innocent in the garden the world had no sterile spots, no noxious weeds, no growth of thorns and thistles. It is enough to be assured that the earth would furnish fertile grounds sufficient for the growing population of mankind; that light labour would have sufficed to secure abundant supplies for the human family; and that no noxious or troublesome growth of thorns and briers would have cumbered the ground. It seems not likely that any new plants were created after the fall of man, and with a special view to vex his labours in tilling the earth. But we know now that weeds grow easily; that even the most unproductive seasons are sufficiently fruitful in them; that they are hard to destroy; and that they greatly increase the toils of the husbandman. The immense abundance of plants for which man has learned no use; their easy spread, and that without cultivation, and even in spite of careful diligence; the sterility of the soil; and perhaps the numerous dangers of frost and drought, of worm and insect, of blight and rot, which fill the life of the husbandman with continual apprehension; may be reckoned among the evils of this first curse.*

These things all enter into the toil of man. As already said, work belonged to him before the fall; even then Adam was the keeper of the garden. But a genial and delightful employment is widely different from a toilsome task; and what we can do cheerfully when no disappointments threaten, when no useless growth supplies the place of that for which we labour, and when we can gather our full sheaves with rejoicing hands, is done with reluctant energy when severer efforts promise a more doubtful issue. The labour of the husbandman is toil, wearing toil, incessant toil. It is made so, not only by the nature of his employment, and the ever recurring necessity, that year by year he must do over again the things already done; but various things make this labour specially toilsome. Sometimes a sterile soil, sometimes imperfect means of cultivation, drought and frost, storm and flood, cutting

* I extract the following from a newspaper, without the means of deciding upon the truth of its extraordinary statements:

ABUNDANCE OF WEEDS.—An English botanist discovered, by careful examination, 7,600 weed seeds in a pint of clover-seed, 12,600 in a pint of congress-seed, 39,440 in a pint of broad clover, and 25,500 of Dutch clover-seed. In a single plant of black mustard he counted over 8,000 seeds, and in a specimen of charlock 4,000; the seed of a single plant of common dock produced 4,700 little docks. The white daisy has over 400 seeds in each flower, and sometimes 50 flowers from one root.

worms and devouring insects, are the disadvantages against which he must labour. Anxiety for the issue of these toils hovers like a dark cloud over every farm house from seed time to harvest, and from harvest to seed time. Every opening spring is full of forebodings for the coming harvest; nor do the repeated answers of providence, usually so much better than the thoughts of man, serve to repress the new fears of every recurring year. It is not simply the hard work of the field that must be included in our thoughts of the labour of cultivating the earth. The solicitude, the watchfulness, the responsibility, the burden of care—all these without remission; all these growing more weighty in ordinary human experience till men no longer have strength to bear them—these and all that they imply, are included in the declaration, "In the sweat of thy face shalt thou eat bread."

We have in this remarkable declaration an important example of the methods of Scriptural teaching. No writing ever given to man says so much in so little compass as the sacred Scriptures. It is the common custom with the inspired writers to select one striking example out of a class of doctrines or duties, and to embody in it the most valuable, important, and instructive principles to govern the entire class. In the ten commandments we have the whole duty of man comprised in a very brief space; and if we take each separate command into consideration, we will find that the mention of one matter of chief importance is designed to include under it every minor matter belonging to the same class with it. Thus idolatry is the worst form of malpractice in the worship of God; disobedience to parents is the worst form of resistance to lawful authority; killing, the worst form of violence to man; and adultery, the worst form of impurity. The law therefore mentions these by name; but it designs to forbid with them every species of iniquity akin to them. So upon the interpretation of the Scriptures themselves, we know that covetousness is idolatry, an unchaste look is adultery, and hatred to a brother is murder. In like manner the Lord's prayer endorses every needful principle for our devotions; and if we consider the particular petitions, we may see that every acceptable petition that man should offer to God may be classified to fall under one or other clause of this sixfold prayer. So there are single parables spoken by our Lord; and single miracles wrought by his power; and single conversions recorded in the Bible; and single sentences uttered by the inspired writers, that may be justly interpreted as including every important principle that is needful to establish the authority and the grace of the gospel, or to give instruction and comfort to sinful men.

Interpreting these solemn words in Eden by this remarkable characteristic of Scriptural teachings, it cannot be called in question that labour and toil belong to the sons of Adam in every age and climate and in every condition of life. The curse is not confined to the mere culture of the earth. This alone is named, not simply because it was the especial employment of Adam, but because there is no other employment in human life upon which man is so dependent. We may certainly say of the cultivation of the earth more than of any other human duty, that it is absolutely essential to man's existence. One single year of sterility and barrenness of the earth's products over all the world would be followed by distress such as the history of man has never seen; and five years without a harvest would leave the world a waste, without seed to sow for coming years and without a man to need it. "The profit of the earth is for all; the king himself is served by the field." Ecc. v. 9. The earth is the common mother of us all; from her products we live; the culture of the ground as the most important kind of labour, is the fitting representative of human toil.

It is not alone the man that tills the earth who feels this first curse of labour. We need not here make any comparisons of men's avocations; or attempt to show that in this or that line of life, the surest success and the largest content will crown our labours. While we may simply and justly acknowledge that honourable, contented, successful, and useful industry may as often be found among men that till the ground as anywhere else on earth; what we now say is that this early curse equally belongs to all other human labours, and, indeed, is inseparable from man's estate. Weary limbs, and heavy hearts, and anxious minds are everywhere upon the earth; painful toils, disappointed hopes, and fruitless efforts form part of every man's experience; sorrow in labour, the sweating of the face, and results like to thorns and thistles are found in all our work. The curse belongs to every trade, every profession, and every time. With the increase of population in every land, especially with the advancement of the race in the arts of civilized life, the engagements of men become more numerous; distinctions of rank and wealth increase in society; some men never tan their faces with the glare of the sun, or harden their hands with the axe or the plough; and some, born to rank and affluence, are clothed in purple and fare sumptuously every day. Yet there is no human abode exempt from the curse of the fall. It is a great mistake to judge that the great Ahasuerus can bar his palace gates against anxiety and sorrow, though he may forbid sackcloth to enter; or that the diamond valve of the rich man's heart never opens at the touch of care. Labour, corroding thoughts, restless anxieties, belong to man. The palace is their abode; they hover over the couch of the wealthy; they intrude into the sleeping and the waking hours of the wise man; they know no distinctions of rank, or place, or power. Indeed among the compensations of Divine Providence which set men substantially more upon a level with each other, it has often been noted that more happiness and less corroding care can be found in those members of society who hold little in possession, than among their richer neighbours. Nor is it simply because men are prone to be troubled by things present, and to look back with regret to the past, that many a rich man is ready to say that he was never more happy than in his earlier days of poverty and cheerful but humble labour.

We may not overlook this, among the great mercies of God, that the sentence thus pronounced in Paradise is not purely a curse. This human toil which Providence has made so inseparable from human life, may still, when controlled by the fear of God and by wise views of human duty, react as a blessing; and no man passes a more miserable life than he who spends his time as an idler. While the rich have their weighty cares as truly as the poor; while he that increaseth substance increaseth sorrow; while through constant solicitude and anxieties, a truly contented man is a rare thing upon the earth, we may bless God that even the curse of labour is not without its aspects of good.

We have no kind of sympathy with those who regard labour as a menial or a degrading thing; we regard it as both unwise and wicked to wish to live without labour; we have no patience with those who grasp after the comforts of life, and yet are ashamed of the honest industry by which these have been secured to them; and we treat that as ignorant folly that would array one class of labourers against another in the arrangements of human society.

There are many proper objects of human industry; not all of equal importance, yet the least important not calling for any contempt; our comparisons, indeed, are likely to be made in ignorance or prejudice. And this is our just rule of judgment: that whatever is useful for man is worthy to be held in honour by man. There is a toil that pales the cheek, and weakens the arm, and wears out this tenement of flesh, as well as a toil that bathes the face in sweat and gives strength to every muscle. And in these times when the busy industry of life in every department of labour owes so much to the inventive genius, and the patient investigation, and the abstract thoughts of studious men, it is too late to draw invidious distinctions between productive and non-productive labour. It is high time that rational men should everywhere recognize that labour and thought are not antagonists; that indeed that is the happiest estate where they best harmonize together; that every man of mechanical labour should love to think for the sake of his mind, and that he may be something more than the horse he drives or the tool he uses; and that every student, for health's sake, and to give vigour to his thoughts, should take wholesome exercise of body. But every man who has an honourable and useful calling, and puts forth in it the energy of a healthful life, deserves to be held in estimation.

The true idea of human society is that of a machine of many parts, a body of many members. All the parts of some complicated mechanism are not of equal importance; yet the movements of a steam engine may be stopped by the breaking of a pin; the safety of a vessel may be put in jeopardy by a flaw in a single nail or rope. In the body, all members have not the same office; yet the suffering of one member is an injury to all; and the prosperity of one member is to the advantage of all. There are idlers among men; there are those who accomplish less than we have reason to expect from them; and there are those whose busy industry is exerted to injure rather than to benefit society. Let these all be judged as they deserve. But let us acknowledge that useful industry, wisely directed in any engagement of life, confers honour and happiness upon men. It would not be better for any man if he could live without labour. Something to do is every man's blessing; and in the Divine mercy even this sentence upon man's sin, is not purely a curse.

CHAPTER XVI.

DEATH.

We pursue further our thoughts upon the facts implied in the curse upon Adam. The sentence of Divine displeasure next speaks of that solemn hour when he should return to the dust from which he had been formed. The tempter's words are vain and false. Man must "surely die."

It is an important inquiry, What is included in that sentence which God now pronounced upon man, as a guilty, fallen creature? That the term *death* includes the dissolution of the bond that unites the soul and the body, and the fall of the body to the earth, is plain from the very words here used. Is this all it means? We may give our thoughts briefly to this matter.

Some persons suppose that man is mortal by the very constitution of his being; and that he would have met with temporal death, and his body would have fallen to the dust, if even he had never sinned. In proof of their view, they argue that the death of the irrational creatures is a necessary part of their conditions of life; that death enters into the arrangements of providence as truly as life; that their succession is apparently needful to the condition of the world; that we have abundant proof that whole races have filled the earth and perished long anterior to any evidence of man's existence upon the globe; and that this body of man is of the dust and corruptible, and ever changing as it tends to the earth again. Yet there are many reasons which prevent us from receiving such views, more powerful than any arguments in their favour. We do not believe in the mortality of man in his first estate of innocence. It is not necessarily true that because death occurred to the irrational creatures, therefore intelligent and rational man was also subject to it: this fleshly body could have undergone the changes needful to fit it for a life in heaven without meeting death; (see 1 Cor. xv. 51;) the actual transition of Enoch and Elijah, at a subsequent period of the history, points out to us an actual way in which all needful changes might occur to man's constitution; and the constant teachings of the Scriptures that death entered by sin, and as the wages of sin, and passed upon all men by reason of sin, seem to forbid that we should entertain any other than the ordinary view.

But while we believe that the race of man would have known no such thing as the fall of the body to the dust, had we remained sinless, we can easily see that the chief element after all of such an event lies in the cause of it. Death is serious, revolting, humiliating; so much so as to form an argument to prove that no such grief would ever have been laid upon the sinless. To breathe out our life; to lay this cherished body down to darkness and corruption; to part thus from those that have been near and dear to us, is no light sorrow, even when alleviated by the hope or the knowledge that the separation is not final. But when we magnify most all the grief of such an event, it must still be confessed that the cause of death is the circumstance of chief aggravation. "The sting of death is sin." Take away the sense of sin unpardoned, and man can look death in the face with composure; or even with triumph conquer this stern foe. There is in human estimation the widest difference between the death of the craven and fiendish Robespierre and that of the noble and patriotic Sir William Wallace, though they both died by the hand of the public executioner. The world looks differently upon them, and these men themselves would feel that the mere publicity of an execution was not its chief shame. The severest pang of death belongs to its nature as a deserved sentence of law. This is the force of the Apostle's word; "The sting of death is sin."

But if the true pang of death lies in its punitive nature, we may justly include under it all the sufferings that have flowed from sin. The separation between our first parents and God; the loss of confidence; the interruption of intercourse; and all the results flowing from sin so long as the creature remains under the displeasure of his Creator, are to be reckoned under this single but comprehensive term, DEATH. As the life promised to obedient Adam included spiritual and eternal well being; so the death threatened was its reverse. Every blessing of God's favour upon man obedient would surely have been the reward of obedience; nor does, nor will man suffer aught in this life, or in that which is to come, in a judicial manner, but as the wages of sin.

God pronounced upon Adam the sentence of which he had been forewarned. From that time, and even from the first moment of transgression, began the curse. The reign of temporal death was soon set up; and how vain is it for us even to imagine the fearful forms in which it has ruled the earth! When death comes in its mildest aspects, and alleviated by the kindest sympathies of human love, it is a sad and serious event. We cannot enter the chamber over which the dark shadow of his approach is already cast; we cannot look upon the victim of death's triumph; we cannot lay away the loved remains in their last resting place, without serious thoughts; and we know that when the time comes for any of us to meet this foe, the conflict will seem as new and strange, as if no man else had ever struggled with this enemy. But in what various forms has death come to the family of man!

In how many sad scenes have we ourselves mingled, as we have entered the house of mourning! We have seen the infant of days, the blooming youth, the vigorous man, and the hoary head of age touched by the stern hand of this unsparing and indiscriminate curse. We have seen his slow approaches by lingering disease, and his rapid stroke by accident or crime. And with the well known population of the world before our eyes, how serious is the thought that with every minute of time death strikes down scores of victims; and that with every hour spent in the sanctuary a larger number of souls than sit with us in the house of mercy have passed into eternity!

> "Ah little think the gay, licentious proud,
> Whom pleasure, pomp, and affluence surround;
> They who their thoughtless hours in giddy mirth,
> And wanton, often cruel, riot waste;
> Ah little think they while they dance along,
> How many feel, this very moment, death,
> And all the sad variety of pain!
> How many sink in the devouring flood,
> Or more devouring flame!"

Who could bear to read the dark and blotted page that should record the scenes of suffering and death that occur all over the earth upon any single day of man's history! And when we multiply these days by years, and these years by centuries, what an appalling aggregate do we bring before us;

and how large seems the fearful curse that was introduced into our world by sin!

Nor should we reckon death only among the woes thus brought upon our earthly existence. We must add with the poet

> " All the thousand nameless ills,
> That one incessant struggle render life
> One scene of toil, of suffering."
> " How many drink the cup
> Of baleful grief, or eat the bitter bread
> Of misery! . . . . . .
> How many shake
> With all the fiercer tortures of the mind,
> Unbounded passion, madness, guilt, remorse!"

For sin brings forth sin; and grief and woe are its sad fruits everywhere.

That is a most serious chapter in the history of man, that a most convincing proof that death and sin stand in close union, which would record the victories of death over man by the hand of his fellow man. How early the reign of violence began! The first born of Adam was the first murderer: and the very words by which human language has classified these deeds of blood—homicide, and regicide, and fratricide, and parricide, and matricide, and infanticide, and suicide—give proof that sin bears its deadly fruits through all the flowing veins of human society. And what can we say of the wars that have desolated the earth, and that with all their bad passions have deluged cities and lands with blood, but that they are the legitimate offspring of the sin of man?

Sin, which has thus widely separated man from innocence and from God, throws its dark shadow forward beyond the life that now is. Surely if death is itself the fruit of sin, the fruit of death cannot be reconciliation to an offended God. If sinful man is still immortal, he is immortal as a sinner; death itself, which is laid upon him as a curse, has no such purifying power as to restore him to his estate of innocence, and to prepare him for the holy and everlasting service of God. We may not only reason thus; we may not only deny that any proof exists that the fall of the body to the earth exhausts the curse of God's broken law; but we may appeal to the more explicit declarations of the subsequent Scriptures. These declare no new sentence of an offended God; but simply interpret in plainer terms the judgments of God against sin. The sinner who bears the curse of death in all the dread meaning of the term, shall never see God's face in peace; shall go away into everlasting punishment; shall never have forgiveness either in this life or in the life to come; shall be punished with everlasting destruction from the presence of the Lord, and from the glory of his power. These are not man's thoughts, without reason, without right, without authority, and without importance. They are the serious declarations of God's inspired prophets; they are spoken more plainly and repeatedly by none than by the incarnate Son of God himself; and they fully justify the usual faith of the church of God, that death temporal, spiritual, and eternal is the wages of man's sin.

CHAPTER XVII.

THE CURSE UPON THE RACE.

"On all his sons
Through every age the sad inheritance
Of sin and death entailed."

HAYES.

IT cannot be called in question that the evils included in the curse of Eden, as thus far considered, were designed to come not only upon our guilty first parents, but also upon all their posterity, "descending from them by ordinary generation." The sorrows and subjection of Eve belong to all her daughters; the earth still brings forth thorns and briers for each new generation; the toil and anxiety of labour yet rests on every man; and death reigns in all the abodes of Adam's children. These things may be justly reckoned among the facts of human history.

And there are other facts which ought to be recognized as such by every candid and observant man. First among them we may reckon the universal sinfulness of the race. This fact has two important aspects which we may distinctly notice. First, it is a truth that men are universally sinners; and second, this sinfulness of the race stands connected with the sin of Adam. So the Scriptures expressly say, "By one man sin entered into the world, and death by sin, and so death passed upon all men for that all sinned." The nature of the connection between the first man and his race shall be the subject of our subsequent investigations. Now we speak simply of the facts in the case; leaving the principles involved in them to those later thoughts.

It seems scarcely necessary to prove that whereever man is, sin is, because no candid and intelligent mind will be disposed to deny the sad fact. Not only are the declarations of the sacred writers explicit upon this point, when they affirm that all flesh is corrupt, that there is none righteous, no, not one, and that there is not a just man upon the earth that doeth good and sinneth not; but there are manifold arguments which may be drawn from our own observation to prove the universality of man's sin.

Dr. Dwight in his System of Theology has a discourse upon this subject in which, after speaking of the testimony of the Scriptures, he adduces these further proofs.

1. The laws of all nations prove the sinful character of man. Laws are chiefly to restrain and punish sin. Necessity forces every nation to adopt

them; to invent severe penalties for crimes; to use all watchfulness against them. Man needs laws, courts, judges, bonds, locks, jails, gibbets, because sin everywhere abounds; and yet in no single nation on the face of the earth have these things ever proved effectual to stop men from sinning. The sinfulness of man is cunning enough to escape the most watchful police; bold enough to dare the severest punishments; deep enough to outlast the longest efforts of reform. All these things have failed to exterminate a single sin. In a virtuous world none of these things would be needed; and their universal existence proves man's universal sin.

2. The religions of all nations prove the same thing. Every system of religion has its ideas of expiation. Whether sacrifices, offerings, pilgrimages, ablutions, or penances, the conscience of man was ever burdened and guilt was ever confessed, where these were found.

3. The writings of all nations, who have had any writings, prove man's universal sin. History, though often partial, has always described man as evil towards God and as unjust and cruel towards man. Moral and philosophical writings, even those that oppose this very doctrine, not to speak of other writings, have yet borne strong testimony to its truth by the very efforts made to disprove it; while all other writings, as poems, and works of fiction, owe all their interest to the just recognition of man's universal wickedness. Men do not care to

read any poem or novel which introduces a perfect character; for such a character is seen at once to be unnatural.

4. The conversation of all men is proof of man's sin. All men charge others with sin, and very few profess themselves sinless. Those who do this gain little credit for their intelligence or sincerity; and the best of men are usually the most humble in acknowledging their shortcomings.

5. The history of the race has failed to record a single instance of a pure and spotless man, with the sole exception of Jesus of Nazareth, the promised Seed of the woman.

6. The doctrine of man's universal sinfulness is proved to every man who examines truly his own character.

Every man has his serious apprehensions concerning his future state; every man knows that he does not perform his whole duty; every man is conscious that he has committed many sins; every man finds many difficulties in refraining from sin and in doing right. Every man would be ashamed to tell his secret thoughts to his nearest friend, and every man knows that he is a sinner before the searching eye of God.

The more fully such arguments are expanded and considered, the more convincing is the dreadful proof that man everywhere is vile. We are a sinful race—sin and misery have always and everywhere abounded upon the earth. The sinfulness of man pertains not alone to one age, but to every age; to one nation, but to every nation; to a few persons in each community, but to every man and through all his life.

This sinfulness of man forms a part of man's very nature. We speak of this as a fact to be recognized, just as we recognize the rational and moral nature of man. No one questions that an infant child is a being of a reasonable nature; and this certainly not because of any exercise of reason on the part of the child. We reckon the child a rational being, because it belongs to a race of rational beings; and because of almost universal experience that in the growth and development of the child, he will prove himself possessed of understanding and will, of affections and conscience. The rare instances of idiotic children have no effect to weaken our conviction that the nature of man is rational. But it is no more true that with the growth of every child we shall find evidence of a rational nature, than that we shall find evidence of a depraved nature. Facts prove that the nature of man is corrupt, as plainly as they prove that man is a moral and reasonable being.

Facts prove that the nature of man is entirely depraved. Many, indeed, object to the doctrine of total depravity, just as they do to all the doctrines pertaining to our union with Adam, through a perversion of the terms used to express them. We do not mean by total depravity that every man is as wicked as he can be. In this sense, even Satan is not totally depraved, since his is an existence of increasing sinfulness. We say a man is a total bankrupt when he is unable to pay his debts; but we can recognize that some bankrupts are far more deeply involved than others. By total depravity we mean the depravity of the entire man —of the soul in all its powers. It is not the depravity of the will, while the conscience is fully faithful to its duty; not the corruption of the affections, while the understanding clearly discerns the truth and the memory is faithful to retain it. But all the powers of the mind are affected by the sinfulness of man. His understanding is darkened; his affections are called forth easily towards evil things; he easily treasures up in his memory corrupt and delusive things; his imagination is easily inflamed by corrupting ideas; his will is prone to every evil. There is no natural disposition on the part of man to love God, or to render righteous obedience to his law. God made him upright. Then his delight was in God; he held communion with him; he knew no bias to evil. When we speak then of total depravity, we mean the entire absence of that righteousness which originally belonged to man, and the corruption of the entire nature, without including the actual transgressions which indeed proceed from this depravity, but which are clearly to be distinguished from it.

It is among the facts of which we now speak, that

the whole nature of man not only falls short of that uprightness in which Adam was created; not only is indisposed to spiritual good, but is made opposite to it; is wholly inclined to all evil; "is very far gone from original righteousness, and is of his own nature inclined to evil." Of this speaks David when he says, Behold, I was shapen in iniquity; and our Lord Jesus when he affirms, That which is born of the flesh is flesh; and Paul, when he declares that the carnal mind is enmity against God. And the solemn and repeated declarations of the Scriptures are confirmed, as we see how averse men are to the spiritual doctrines of the gospel; how many constant restraints are needful to keep even children from forming the most corrupt habits; how easy, we may expressively say, how *natural* is every evil thing among the children of men! We acknowledge that there is great diversity in human wickedness. The length of life and the number of their transgressions may be greater in some men than in others. All men are alike in this, that all are averse from God and prone to evil; but the progress made in evil is quite a different matter.

We speak of these things as facts in the history of man, and we do not now attempt to give any explanation of them; to enter, as men would say, upon the philosophy of these matters. This indeed it is our privilege to do; this we design to do. We believe that the facts are furnished us in order to the just understanding of the truth upon the principles of sound philosophy. Let us now simply endeavour to notice a few things which enter into the process of such a philosophy.

1. It is acknowledged by the wisest men that all sound philosophy consists in observing and classifying all the facts of any subject; and from these facts to learn the principles from which the facts arise. It is not for us to invent, but to discover laws. Nor is it always an easy thing to reduce all the observed facts into entire consistency with each other. Yet the facts are right; and the apparent inconsistency between them must be attributed to ignorance, or inexperience and want of wisdom on the part of the philosopher.

2. The facts of which we now speak are plainly true in the history of man, and lie open to the notice of every one. It is injustice to this subject to allege that only those who receive the Scriptures as the word of God are bound to believe these things. The Scriptures do speak explicitly on these topics; and their utterances should indeed be satisfactory to every Christian. Yet it is just for us to say that all these facts of man's condition depend upon no line of historical proof, even as handed down in the church of God; but every man may see them before his own eyes. They rest not upon the truth of the Bible or of the Christian religion; but they force themselves upon the notice of those who profess any religion or none. That the Bible

declares any truth, does not prevent us from noticing the independent proofs of it from other sources. These facts connected with the sinfulness and misery of man's estate must be noticed by every observant mind; and let a man's religious opinions be what they may, his philosophy should embrace these facts, and give some explanation of them.

3. We are not to expect that any explanation of these difficulties will be perfectly satisfactory. Indeed, philosophers, who are wise in the affairs of this world, assure us that a full explanation of any thing is an impossibility. A professedly scientific journal, having the largest circulation and influence, and perhaps the highest practical ability of any in this country, in a recent editorial holds this language: "Nothing can be fully explained. In every department of knowledge, if we go a few steps from that which is visible upon the surface, we come to absolute mystery, which no man can explain. Ask the most learned surgeon to explain the motion of the hand. He tells you," . . . . of the muscles, and nerves, and brain; but "if you ask him how the brain acts upon the nerve, and the nerve upon the muscle, he can tell you no more than can the smallest child or the most ignorant savage. What the nervous influence is . . . . is known to God, but it is not known by any of the children of men." And after illustrative expressions, the conclusion of the writer is: "If we attempt to understand tho-

roughly any fact whatever which comes under our observation, we shall find that a few steps will bring us to the dark gulf of profound and unfathomed mystery."*

If these are unquestioned truths of human philosophy in regard to natural sciences, much less may we expect fully to understand those far more difficult matters which link the mind and soul of man to the spiritual and eternal world. It is presumption for any man to suppose that he can clear a topic like this of all its difficulties. When we learn all we can of these deep things of man's sinfulness, we will still be unable to explain what we may much desire to know.

4. What then we judge is this: That the explanation which we receive from the sacred Scriptures respecting the sin of man, in its origin, and in all its aspects and bearings, is the very simplest, clearest, and most satisfactory that has ever been proposed; at the same time that it stands connected with other teachings the most excellent that man has ever received. The lessons we receive from the word of God do not solve all the difficulties which occur to our mind; but there are less difficulties attending the true solution than any other. And especially we may say that the signal clearness with which the Apostle Paul illustrates the great subject of man's salvation, not only sets

* Scientific American, Nov. 5, 1859.

clearly before our minds the true Scriptural doctrine concerning the sinfulness of man, but may lead us to rejoice in the infinite wisdom of Divine providence and grace, which we may trace both in man's ruin and his recovery.

CHAPTER XVIII.

PRELIMINARY STATEMENTS.

We have before this had occasion to draw the line of distinction between the true teachings of these earlier records, and the knowledge drawn from them by those who at first received them. We do not profess to know how much Adam, or Moses, or David, or any Old Testament believer understood of the truths revealed to them; but we judge of these things much as we do of the knowledge of man in other than religious things. It is one thing to trace the progress of human opinions in any science; and, however interesting this may be, it is another, and a far better thing, to comprehend that science, as we enjoy better opportunities for learning what it really teaches. In regard to the science of Astronomy, we cannot doubt that the laws and phenomena of the heavenly bodies were the same before the eyes of Adam as before our eyes; and thus all the true teachings of the starry heavens were entirely consistent as he saw them with what we learn in later times. The earth revolved around the sun; eclipses occurred as regularly; the laws of gravitation, of electricity, of light, were the same; the forces that exist now existed then; and God wrought before and around men just as he does now. If we had the account of an eclipse clearly and plainly recorded as occurring five thousand years ago, our astronomers would receive the facts as true. But the ancient astronomer who could be trusted for what he saw, did not understand the true principles of the science as they are understood now; and therefore our astronomers from the same sight would gain far more true knowledge. If even we say that the invention of the telescope has been like a new revelation of the starry worlds, enabling the earthly observers to discern more clearly what the skies reveal; yet even the telescope has not contradicted any of the teachings which the heavens had before given. We see new stars; we see the same stars, that men formerly saw, with greater clearness; we have many misapprehensions corrected; but we can justly say that the telescope has revealed no inconsistencies between the earlier and the later teachings of the starry heavens.

What the telescope is to astronomy the New Testament is to religion; in part a revelation of new things; in part a clearer exposition of facts and principles as old as the knowledge of man.

Now, while it is a great thing for men to understand the profound principles of the works and ways of God, it is interesting to reflect that the ordinary benefits derived by man from his works and providence depend less than we often think upon the depths of man's philosophy. The knowledge of man now is greater than in former ages. Man has investigated the phenomena of light; understands many of its laws, its beautiful refractions, and its importance to growth and life; yet doubtless the light was as pleasant to Adam, the rainbow as beautiful to Noah, and the scenery as delightful in Canaan to Abraham and David as to any of their wiser children since. Modern chemistry has analyzed our food, investigated the elementary principles of the various kinds, and told us the nutritive properties they severally possess; and yet we cannot doubt that food tasted as sweet and proved just as nourishing to men who never heard of chemistry; as now indeed the child or the fool can enjoy life along side of the wisest man. The ignorant, who know nothing of philosophy, can use the laws of philosophy to much the same practical advantage as those who give their careful study to these things; indeed the wisest men are constantly using principles they do not comprehend; and it is through the use of them we learn to know them.

Men use abundantly the laws they do not understand. We do not undervalue knowledge; but the sun shines as clearly upon those who do and those who do not understand astronomy; the air breathes as healthfully to those who can and those who cannot analyze it; and human governments are valuable alike to the statesman who can argue learnedly upon their great principles, and to the humblest citizen who cannot argue about them. The blood coursed as freely through every man's veins for thousands of years before its circulation was discovered; the law of gravitation has been the same since God made the worlds, but the solution of a thing so simple and so often seen as the fall of an acorn to the earth, is but very recent in the world's history. But there is no need to multiply illustrations.

Knowledge is excellent. But men have always known facts better than they have known principles; they learn principles from facts; they have always used principles they did not comprehend; and they may enjoy privileges they have never thought about.

When we affirm that the earliest teachings of any science are the same as the later teachings, it is no objection that men have only understood these things lately. Nor is it any objection to the true teachings of religion in any age that we comprehend them only by the aid of the later portions of God's word. The true question in regard to biblical instruction is not, How far does this man or that, how far has this age or that, understood these teachings? But the true inquiry is, What does the word of God teach us? And the meaning of any one passage is consistent with the meaning of every other. Genesis and Revelation are alike inspired. Moses may not be as clear as Paul, but he is as truthful. The morning star may not be as bright to the naked eye; we may not see its phases; but the telescope gives only a clearer vision of the same things.

The plain facts in the history of Adam and in regard to our connection with him, have passed in brief review before us; and these same facts have been before the eyes of men in all ages since our first father's apostasy. God pronounced a solemn sentence upon Adam for his sin; the curse has been upon his natural posterity from that day to this; the facts are apparent before the eyes of all men; the philosophy of the case may have been understood more or less distinctly by different men. It is our place to use all the light we can secure from every quarter, to understand the connection between Adam and his children, which demands or justifies that these evils should rest on more than himself.

The simple solution of the matter is here. Adam stood in Paradise, not in his personal but in a public and representative character. Bearing towards his natural posterity the relation of a representative, his act was legally their act; they are held liable for what he did; and judgment has passed upon them to condemn them. In the language of theology his sin is imputed to them—laid to their account.

This is a subject where many objections arise from mere misapprehension. It may, therefore, be wise to delay the exposition and proof of the true doctrine, that we may spend a little time in giving definitions of several things. Thus we may correct in advance various errors into which men are prone to fall; and may greatly simplify our subsequent thoughts.

CHAPTER XIX.

DEFINITION OF TERMS.

THE COVENANT OF WORKS is the name given to that arrangement made by God with Adam in Paradise, when he forbade him to eat of the tree of the knowledge of good and evil; and promised life as the reward of his obedience. The form of covenant differs from the form of law; not in its obligations, for Adam was as truly bound to obedience to God before the covenant was made and after it was broken, as he was during its continuance. The covenant was a privilege. Though Adam was bound to obedience in everything and perpetually; and though his perfect obedience under law could not have merited the high rewards of heaven, by this covenant God promised that upon his obedience in one very plain and very easy thing, and, perhaps, for a very limited space of time, we should secure the blessings of life eternal. We call this a covenant because it differs from a law; because it has all the characteristics of a covenant in contracting parties, terms, privileges, and penalties; because we understand the prophet Hosea especially to say that Adam transgressed the covenant, Hos. vi. 7; and because we shall see that nothing else than this can satisfy the representations of the Scriptures concerning it. It is called the covenant of works, because obedience was demanded by its terms, and had Adam remained obedient he would have fulfilled its requirements. So it is long afterwards interpreted: "The man that doeth these things shall live by them."

We say Adam was our FEDERAL HEAD. The word "federal" is derived from the Latin *fœdus*, a covenant, and means the same as covenant. Adam was the representative of his children in this covenant. The United States government is called the federal government, and its courts are called federal courts, because the general government of this country exists by a compact or covenant between the states united in its support. Hence the motto, *E pluribus Unum; i. e.*, from many one. Many independent governments unite to form one.

Adam was the federal head of his children for the purposes designed under the covenant of works, in precisely the same sense that an officer of the federal government, acting in his public capacity for the ends entrusted to him, represents the people of the United States. The laws of Congress, made in accordance with the Constitution of the United States, which is the rule of our national covenant, bind the citizens of this entire land, because made by our representatives. And it is even true that the acts of private citizens against foreign governments without any authority are attributed to this government, and we are held responsible until we expressly disavow their acts. Any man intelligent in political history can easily remember facts which illustrate this matter.

The results of Adam's sin come upon us, we are accustomed to say, by the imputation of his guilt. Two words in this expression need to be explained, for they are frequently misunderstood and are subject to frequent misrepresentations.

When we say that we partake of the *guilt* of Adam's first sin, we do not mean the absurd things, that this sin was committed by us in our own persons; that we are personally blameworthy for an act of whose commission we had no possible consciousness; or that we ought to feel for his sin the same remorse and self-reproach we should feel for our own. Much less could it be true that the transfer of his guilt to us leaves him holy. We simply mean that we are held responsible for his sin, in precisely the same sense that a constituent is held responsible for the acts of his representative; a principal, for the acts of his agent or attorney. We may often feel humiliation and grief; we may often suffer for acts we did not do, and for which we cannot feel remorse. If a man possesses property in a distant city, his agent may neglect it, make foolish contracts respecting it, or act in a dishonest manner respecting its income; to the great grief, displeasure, and injury of the owner. The owner cannot reflect upon himself for these acts, as if he himself had done them; but if this man was truly his agent, and how he became so is not the present subject of discussion, he is liable to suffer for all he has done. All the old theologians use the word *reatus*, guilt, in this simple sense of liability to suffer punishment.

Allied to this is the sense in which we use the word *imputation*. We mean that the penalty of the first sin of Adam is laid to our account. It is particularly to be noticed, that the transference of Adam's personal character, so far from meaning the same thing as imputation, is widely different and, indeed, contradictory. If by the imputation of Adam's sin is meant the transfer of his sinfulness, then of course his sinfulness being taken away, he is innocent and we blameworthy. Nobody ever held such a doctrine as this!

We shall have further occasion to illustrate the true meaning by referring to Christ and his sufferings for our sins upon the cross. Suffice it now to say that when we affirm that Christ bore our sins in his own body, we do not mean that their blameworthiness came upon him, and that the spotless Son of God was a sinner. This is abhorrent to all our thoughts. But we do mean that the punishment of our sins was upon Christ; that they were reckoned to his account, and that our representative was a sufferer. Imputation refers, not to qualities and acts, but to legal responsibility.* The personal act of any man is his own; the blame must belong to himself; but the consequences of his acts, whether for suffering or privilege, may come upon others through him. "To impute sin," says an old writer,† "is to charge it upon us, so as legally to inflict deserved punishment. We do not mean that the sin is reckoned to be committed by us; for we did not commit it, but Adam; but it is so reckoned ours upon our being included in him as our covenant head, that we are punished for it according to the demerit of the sin."

* J. M. Mason, iii. 170.

† Hayward's Sermons (1758), p. 15.

CHAPTER XX.

WHENCE THE AUTHORITY OF A REPRESENTATIVE?

When we speak of Adam as our representative, we are not using strange language invented by metaphysical theologians, and applicable only to the mysteries of religion. The principles involved in this relation are as old as the history of man, are of vital importance as the foundation of all human government, and are essential to all social organization. No family, tribe, or government can exist without involving the principles of covenants, of representation, and of imputation, at least in their chief elements.

We do not understand that Adam was the representative of his race in the same sense in which a father represents his children. Adam was our natural father; but in a special sense, as we shall duly notice, he was our federal head in the covenant of works. Yet from the fact that every father does represent his children, and they derive injuries and advantages from his conduct, we may, from the paternal relation, derive an illustration of the place held by Adam. Every representative possesses powers to bind his constituents; these powers are to be interpreted according to the place he holds and the duties assigned him. A child may represent the family for certain things entrusted to him; the father of a family, in his proper sphere as a parent, legitimately acts for all the rest. The extent of a representative's powers is one thing; the principle of representation is distinct from the question of powers.

The principle of representation is just, wise, useful, and necessary in human affairs. Every civil government is and must be representative in its nature. Certain persons act for the nation; by their acts of wisdom the people are benefitted; for their acts of folly a nation is held responsible. And, although in the wickedness of man, gross abuses of this principle of representation abound, and enormous evils have come from it, it is neither safe nor possible to repudiate or reject the principle itself. Human affairs could not move on; nor could society exist without it. Founded in man's nature by God's wisdom, we are obliged to recognize it.

But when we admit the truth that representation is essential to human affairs, it still remains proper for us to inquire, By what authority does any person act in that capacity? If we admit Adam's authority as a parent, how are we to ascertain his authority to act in a capacity which surpasses that of our natural head?

Perhaps the chief objection made to the doctrine that Adam, under the covenant of works, was the representative of his posterity arises from the fact that he was not the chosen representative of his constituents. The basis of the objection is the claim that a just representation implies that the constituents should have a voice in selecting their representative. Of course this was impossible in the case of Adam. It is important to examine this matter, and to inquire if indeed representatives cannot otherwise have just authority.

There is scarcely any more difficult question pertaining to man's social estate and the science of human government, than that which determines upon what foundation rests the just authority which allows one man to act as the representative of others. It is acknowledged upon all hands, that the true basis of all true government is Divine authority. When the infinitely wise and just Creator speaks, it cannot be possible that injury or injustice should result to the rights of man. But the administration of human governments is committed to man; and while men should ever obey the Divine laws and regard justice and truth, constitutions may justly be formed and rulers and representatives may be chosen by men, to carry out the Divine ordinance of government. These things are entirely consistent. God ordains government; but surely that is a clear right in any ruler, and that a valid authority in any constitution, that they exist by the free choice of the people they govern. And liberty will exist among a people in proportion as they guard carefully and jealously against the encroachments which men in the exercise of power have ever been prone to make against the rights of the commonwealth and for their own aggrandizement.

We have nothing to say against the doctrine, considered with its just limitations, that the just authority of human governments and human rulers and representatives arises from the consent of the governed. Yet many serious and difficult questions arise from the fact that the consent of the governed is a thing so partial in its very best estate.

Nobody contends, for example, that the *unanimous* voice of the people of any state is necessary for the election of a governor; yet is he the lawful ruler, even of those who voted *against* him. Still less will any one affirm that the voices of the women and children and resident aliens of the land, are necessary parts of a popular election; and yet their rights, and duties, and interests are as truly affected by every election as are those of any voters. Still less again will any one claim that the generations to come must be consulted in the choice of our rulers now; and yet the generations to come may feel, more than we do, the influence of the things done in our time.

Look then at the state of the case as it appears from one simple illustration. In electing the President of the United States, a very small proportion of those whom his acts may bind, can justly be said to give their consent to his election. If the population is thirty millions, three millions may actually cast their votes. If he has a popular majority of two hundred thousand the case would stand thus: His acts bind legally and righteously the rights, duties, and interests of one million six hundred thousand who voted *for* him; of one million four hundred thousand who voted *against* him; of twenty-seven millions living in the land who were not consulted at all; and the influence of his ignorance or wisdom, his neglect or activity, may pass down to the untold millions who are yet to dwell in this land, and who, of course, could have no voice in constituting him their legal representative.

Thus it may be seen that, when the popular choice is exercised in the best possible manner towards our representatives, it is but very partially true that the choice of those whose interests are affected is necessary to their just authority. In the family relation this choice is never exercised at all; the father is the head of the family by the appointment of Divine providence; and yet, in his proper sphere, he represents his children as truly, and he exercises authority as legitimately, as any ruler on earth.

In large societies, the choice of a governor never means the unanimous consent of all the governed; but always the vote of a majority. It never includes the votes of females and minors, who do not consent at all, or do so by tacit acquiescence or through the votes of others. It never means the consent of posterity; although their dearest rights and interests may be affected by the things done before they were born. And the persons affected by the acts of a representative may be innumerably greater than those who had any voice in selecting him.

Thus we may gather from the arrangements of society and our common ideas of justice, that the exercise of choice in an interested constituency does not enter so essentially as has often been thought, into the elements of just representation. The righteous relation of constituent and representative often exists where consent is impossible; often where consent is not unanimous; often where dissent is plainly expressed. There may be other things demanded; and their presence may more than compensate for the absence of that general consent which is forbidden by the circumstances of the case. If it must be admitted that succeeding generations may be held responsible for the promises, and engagements, and acts of those now living, then the most important difficulty of the case is really disposed of. Adam might as rightfully act for his successors as we for ours, so far as pertains to this particular matter, the consent of the parties interested.

Nor is it possible for us to imagine a better *right to act* in this capacity than that which flows from *the Divine appointment.* As the authority of a parent flows from Divine Providence; as this appointment is easily ascertained; and as no authority is more legitimate in its proper sphere; so any authority granted from the Divine government should be unquestioned for its legitimacy, its justice, and its excellence. In ordinary representation in human governments, the difficulty lies in deciding *what constitutes the proof of Divine approval. Government is of God* is a great truth. *Is this ruler legitimate?* is quite another question. But certainly if it can be made to appear that Adam acted, not as a private person, but as the head of the human race; the very fact itself is a sufficient proof that his just authority so to do, proceeded from the only source then possible. God either gave him this authority, or recognized his right to exercise it. Unless, then, we are ready to charge evil upon the God of unchangeable wisdom, holiness, and goodness, we must not only lay aside our untenable and inconsistent objections; we must not only be content to believe where we do not clearly see; but we must recognize the *proof of the fact* in such a case as the *proof of right;* and say if Adam was regarded as a covenant head in the eye of God, he was not wrongfully so.

CHAPTER XXI.

THE COVENANT MADE WITH ADAM — REASONABLE ARGUMENTS.

A REPLY to the inquiry, Did God indeed form a covenant with Adam as the root and representative of the human race? may now form the subject of several chapters.

Affirming the existence of such a covenant, the following are some of the reasons we would assign for our faith.

The first reason is this: Such an arrangement, in itself considered, is worthy of the wisdom of God and of his goodness towards man; and it was made on terms highly advantageous to the human family.

The constitution of the human race, as descending from one pair and as moral and reasonable beings, was devised in God's infinite wisdom. All our just reasonings, therefore, upon this entire topic, must be based upon man, not as we think he should have been, but as God made him. Surely we have not knowledge or wisdom enough to say, that any other constitution for the race was preferable. God pronounced Adam very good; and this approval would have extended to all the race so long as it remained sinless. He must be presumptuous indeed, who goes so far back as to find fault with the very nature given by God to the human family.

As God made Adam he was a moral and rational being; and his children were all to partake of the same nature with their first father. By the necessity of such a nature, each individual is under obligations of personal, perfect, and perpetual obedience to the entire law of God. We cannot conceive that a moral being could ever rightfully disobey the will of the wise and holy God, his Creator. But the utmost perfection of obedience could not bring the Divine Ruler under any obligations to bestow special rewards upon the creature. Law never rewards obedience, in the strict sense of reward. A just God could not punish an innocent being; he would bestow his favour upon an obedient creature as he did to Adam during his entire estate of innocence. But by obedience to the law of God no creature could merit that exceeding weight of glory which we are taught to call by the name of HEAVEN. If Adam and his race had inherited the original conditions of their being, they would have been under law alone and for ever. *Perhaps* they would have been for ever liable to fall. Certainly their continued obedience would have secured for them but the favour of God, without any legal claims upon higher rewards which no services of the creature can merit.

Now a covenant wonderfully changes this estate of man. Instead of making his obedience have regard to the entire law, it confines the trial of his faithfulness to one single self-denial; and this the very simplest and easiest of performance that Divine benevolence could require of him. Instead of making his obedience perpetual for himself and for his race, with, perhaps, the constant liability to fall through all their lives, we have every reason to judge that he and all his race, after a short period of trial, would have been confirmed in holiness and happiness for ever. Every free creature is, perhaps, liable to fall, considered simply as to his natural powers; but the grace of God can confirm holy beings in holiness beyond the possibility of fall; which case now belongs to the saints and angels in glory. Instead of making his obedience depend on law without special promises, the great promises of everlasting life were set before him. And these preferable things offered by Divine goodness to Adam, in exchange for his natural condition under law, were hampered by no such disadvantages as to make the covenant injurious or burdensome. The penalty was no more severe for breaking the covenant than the natural exposedness of the creature under the law; for the disobedience of a creature, in any particular and at any time, would have met the same displeasure of God. Nor have we any just reason to say that without such a covenant each individual of the race would have been subjected to a temporary probation. If God had left us under mere law, our service must have been for all our duties, of perpetual requirement and with no special promises for obedience. Or if he had formed a covenant for each, the likelihood of obedience could never be stronger than in the garden.

The truth is, the covenant of works made by God with Adam was an exceedingly great and valuable privilege bestowed by the just and benevolent Creator upon the newly formed race. Unless we question the whole foundation of man's natural and moral estate—though the product of infinite wisdom—we cannot gainsay the truth of this. It was incomparably better that man should be under a temporary covenant than that he should remain in his natural estate under a perpetual law; that he should have the early hope of confirmation in holiness rather than the constant liability to fall; that one simple and easy requirement should take the place of the numerous and perplexing claims of duty under the whole law; that while the penalty was not increased, the rewards of obedience should be so large in exchange for the natural advantages flowing from God's justice under the law towards obedient persons. To exchange the natural estate of man for this brief covenant, to make Adam responsible in the full maturity of his powers, with the consciousness of his trust, and with so great easiness of obedience, is not a transaction chargeable with folly and injustice. If Adam had but stood the trial, the gratitude of the race would have been unbounded; both to our first father for his success, and to the blessed God for the goodness that gave man the opportunity of securing everlasting life by means so simple and easy. Unless, then, we are guilty of the wickedness of charging the fault of the failure upon God, which is entirely untrue; we ought to recognize, not only that he did thus enter into covenant with Adam, but that infinite wisdom and goodness prompted the arrangement. The covenant would have succeeded but for man's sin; its success would have been glorious; and the mere fact of failure, however disastrous, does not invalidate its excellent principles; and should bring no reproach upon its holy and benevolent Author.

A second reason for our faith may be drawn from its reasonableness; not only in itself, but as compared with other attempts to explain the whole subject.

The most serious difficulties upon this entire matter confessedly attend any view whatever that will include the well known facts; and every important objection is quite as hard to meet in any view we may take. But it is a settled principle of sound philosophy that objections to well established facts are of no weight. Facts give knowledge, objections arise out of our ignorance. Their true cure is, not the denial of what we already know, but to learn more. And we must expect to find in the teachings of the Scriptures the same difficulties we find in the world about us; since they have the same Author.* As already said, we cannot fully explain anything even in natural science. Perhaps in religious teachings there is this additional reason for obscurity; that God especially demands humility and faith in every worshipper; and the clouds and darkness around some interesting subjects of thought may the better secure his purpose.

Men are greatly tempted to charge God with injustice to the race in this matter. The Almighty vindicates himself from this charge most explicitly; but not by clearing up the difficulties which men cannot solve. He declares the infinite and unchangeable holiness of his own character; explicitly avows that he tempts no man to evil, that he judges righteous judgment of every man; and that the blame of man's sin and ruin in no sense attaches to Him; and calls upon man, in view of plain truth and in spite of ignorance in some things, to believe that the Divine throne is spotless. Whatever seeming contradictions there may be, let *faith* acknowledge that there is no real inconsistency. Because a feeble worm cannot explain the mysterious dealings of God, it does not follow that they are inexplicable. For he may make the darkest bright in the day of his revelation. For the present he

* Origen quoted by Bishop Butler.

often says, "What I do thou knowest not now, but thou shalt know hereafter."

Bearing in mind that the chief difficulties of this case are common to every view man can get of it, we may proceed to speak of some theories which seem to us less satisfactory than the sentiments we have expressed.

Some have supposed that the facts of man's universal sinfulness can be accounted for, by acknowledging that every man is possessed of a voluntary nature, and that by the exercise of his own free will every man chooses the ways and thoughts of evil. Others have thought that the evil examples everywhere existing in the world are a sufficient explanation of universal sinfulness. But it is utterly incredible that, in the exercise of free will in moral beings entirely unbiassed by evil, among so many millions of individuals through the ages of time, there never should occur one single instance of the choice of good. Surely if the will of man *was* perverted and prone to wrong, the fatal tendency could not be worse than well known results really are. And it is just as inexplicable, that bad examples should be invariably copied by beings, who, but for these, would be holy. For there are many good examples set before the children of our race; and bad examples ought, at least in some cases, to serve as warnings and to deter, rather than win, a mind that has no bias to evil. And the mystery in the providence of God is not at all relieved if we deny that man is corrupt by nature, and yet affirm that he is placed in circumstances where every individual is sure to become corrupt.

Others have recognized all the evils of a corrupt nature as flowing from the sin of the first man; but they refuse to recognize the existence of the covenant of works, and declare that men inherit the curse upon Adam by reason of a Divine constitution to that effect. Whatever in such a theory is different from the doctrine of Adam's federal headship, relieves us of no difficulty; while serious disadvantages are involved to which just objection may be made. By this arbitrary Divine constitution to which even Adam is not supposed to give consent, the human race never had any trial, nor any favourable opportunity of securing everlasting life; we are not otherwise connected with Adam than as our first father, nor was he divinely appointed to act for us; yet, by virtue of this Divine constitution, all these evils come upon us for the sin of one, with whom, upon this theory, we had no special connection. While this view relieves no difficulty, it involves more serious ones. It bids us believe that without any union with Adam we suffer just the same as if we had been united to him; and, moreover, it seems necessarily to forbid that the obedience of Adam would have been of any special service to his posterity. Had the first man obeyed the special command of God, his children would not have suffered these evils; but neither would they have "reigned with him in life." They would still have been under law, and perhaps each one in a state of trial for himself, and for aught we know, with the perpetual liability to fall.

But if we believe there was a covenant, then good on the one hand and evil on the other, depended upon the obedience of our representative, until the time had expired and the terms of the covenant were fulfilled. If we believe that Adam was only under law, and this not in a covenant form; if his obedience was merely personal; if it must be perpetual; if no time was promised of confirmation in holiness, such as now belongs to the angels and saints in heaven; and if every one of his children must stand precisely in this position, then this supposed Divine constitution puts the entire human family under the most serious disadvantages, without any attempt to explain the Divine rectitude and without a redeeming promise of good, such as vindicates the Divine benevolence in the covenant of works.

Believe in a covenant, and Adam's position is not personal but public; the largest blessings are promised to his seed upon easy terms; a person eminently fit stands for them; and the evils of his unhappy failure come upon more than himself because of a legal connection.

Here then is a brief summary of these thoughts. The facts already considered compel us to believe that the race of man is corrupt; the universality of this corruption forbids us to decide that it can be accounted for by anything short of a depraved nature in the entire race. And if we must choose between an arbitrary Divine constitution, based upon no well known principles, promising no advantages, and bringing innumerable evils through Adam upon those who stood towards him in no special connection; and a covenant which places for our representative, a man of all others the most suitable for place and capacity; which promises extraordinary advantages upon his obedience; and which upon principles that radically belong to our social nature, makes us liable to the results of his disobedience, through our legal union and connection with him, the choice between those two explanations seems easily made. The covenant made with Adam seems every way the simplest solution of the matter. There are some difficulties that are not removed by this view; but not one existing difficulty is magnified; no new, especially no superior, difficulties are created; this harmonizes with other things in human experience, in the dealings of God's providence and in the teachings of the Scriptures; and not least of all, as we shall see, this explanation finds its glorious counterpart in that greater covenant by which the grace of God repairs the ruins of the fall.

CHAPTER XXII.

THE COVENANT MADE WITH ADAM—FURTHER PROOF FROM SCRIPTURE.

THE narrative in Genesis, scarcely capable of any other solution, forms a third reason for affirming the existence of the covenant of works.

Here God and Adam stand towards each other in relations different from that of the mere creature before his Creator. As in a covenant, we have two parties before us; on the one hand, God; on the other, mankind, in the person of the only living member of the race then in existence. Here are terms. The natural and inalienable duty of every creature is perpetual and entire obedience. But here, evidently for some special purpose, God substitutes a requirement incomparably less difficult. How small a thing was it to require that a holy being should refrain from the fruit of a single tree, when he was so fully supplied with the necessaries and even the luxuries of life! How impossible it is to understand why such evident importance should be attached to this command, if no special privilege was included under it! Any duty of

Adam's life was a test of personal obedience; this must be a special test for special purposes and with special privileges. Here are sanctions. The penalty of man's disobedience was natural and necessary; no creature could with impunity sin against God. But here the penalty is specially extended to an act that in itself was harmless; and which became exceedingly sinful just because of the especial place which that forbidden tree held in a dispensation that differed from the moral law. And more than the mere approbation of God upon innocence is plainly implied in the blessings which were thus promised to obedient men. Here also we have the consent of the man fairly implied; given in the words of Eve to the serpent; included in the utter absence of complaint on the part of Adam, as to this point, after he had fallen and the sentence was pronounced upon his disobedience. Our first parents in the first discovery of their sin did murmur against God; but they have, even in their sin, not a word to say against a sentence that can only be explained, in its far reaching influence, by the existence of a covenant.

We regard it as a fourth argument that the formation of such a covenant with Adam corresponds not only with the nature of man, but with the usual methods of God's dealings with the sons of men.

From the beginning of the Bible, through all its pages, we have frequent mention made of an everlasting covenant, made with God's people and with their seed. We have no direct account of the formation of this covenant or of its first proclamation as a covenant to man. When first spoken of in the Scriptures, it is introduced as a privilege whose nature and terms were already well understood. From the time that he said to Noah, "Behold, I establish *my covenant* with you and with your seed after you," Gen. ix. 9; we find mention made of this covenant, and of its extension to future generations, in all the Scriptures. It is not only with Abraham and Jacob, and with Israel at Sinai that God made this covenant; but God's covenant, the everlasting covenant, is mentioned in the histories, in the psalms, and in the prophecies of the Old Testament; and in the New Testament, Zacharias prophesied of it at the birth of John the Baptist, Luke i. 72; Peter preached of it at Pentecost; and Paul argued upon it against the errors of the early Church, Gal. iii.

It makes no difference to our present argument, whether we regard these expressions as denoting the same covenant, proclaimed even in the family of Adam after the fall with the solemn rite of sacrifice for its seal, having no early records of its express terms, but explained in all the subsequent Scriptures; or whether we suppose that these frequent terms denote different covenants, made with Noah, Abraham, Israel, and David. Nor need we, at present, distinguish between the spiritual benefits of the covenant kept, and the judgments of God for the covenant broken. The simple points of present remark are, that God has repeatedly covenanted with man; and that he ever includes in the covenant the children of those with whom the covenant was made. He included Noah and his seed; Abraham and his seed; David and his seed; and at Sinai it was said to the people, "Neither with you only do I make this covenant, but with him that is not here with us this day." And if we follow the history of the people of Israel through all the Bible, we will find them punished by the judgments of God for the breach of the covenant made with their fathers so long before. Not only so, we may lift up our eyes now and see the Jews a scattered and a suffering people in all the earth, because of the sins of their fathers eighteen centuries ago, against a covenant that is at least three thousand years old. We have ample proof then that the covenant made with Adam binding his posterity to the latest generation is entirely according to God's usual dealings with the sons of men.

We may derive a fifth reason and the strongest, and most explicit of all, from the direct teachings of the Scriptures.

We are expressly informed that the evils of sin and death come upon us through Adam. We need to examine but a few of the more direct passages.

In Hosea vi. 7 we read, "But they like men have transgressed the covenant." The original Hebrew is, "They *like Adam* have transgressed the covenant;" and the same phrase is so rendered in Job xxxi. 33. This is a direct affirmation of the covenant made with Adam.

In 1 Cor. xv. 22 the apostle says expressly, "In Adam all die." This cannot mean less than that we die by reason of Adam's sin. But what he says in Rom. v. 12—21 is still more explicit. As we have other things to say of this passage, we may now simply appeal to these repeated statements: —By one man sin entered into the world and death by sin; through the offence of one many be dead; by one man's offence death reigned by one; by the offence of one judgment came upon all men to condemnation; by one man's disobedience many were made sinners.

Now from the teachings of the fifth chapter of Romans we may draw two further arguments to prove that Adam stood as our representative in the covenant of works.

The first is from the force of the apostle's argument from the death of infants. We have no reason to think that death comes upon one portion of the human family for one reason, and that it comes upon other portions for other and different reasons. If any portion of the race dies because Adam sinned, then it is equally righteous that others should die for the same reason. It is disputed whether the apostle does or does not refer to infants when he speaks of them that "had not sinned after the similitude of Adam's transgression." It is of no importance to the force of our present argument, whether he refers to them or not. For since infants "who have neither done good nor evil," Rom. ix. 11, do die and have died since the world began, an argument framed exactly in the words of Paul is applicable to them; and is unanswerable to prove that their death proves their condemnation under the law. Study the death of an infant child; acknowledge that it has not personally sinned; believe according to the teachings of the Bible that suffering and death are the proofs of a broken law and the wages of sin; but while you see that here are pain, and suffering, and death, and the return of the body to the dust, you multiply the mysteries that becloud all reasonings upon such a subject, unless you receive this solution, that death comes upon them, and if upon them as well upon all men, through the sin of a broken covenant. The well known epitaph expresses the whole matter.

"Bold infidelity, turn pale and die!
Beneath this stone two infants' ashes lie;
Say—are they lost or saved?
If death's by sin, they sinned because they're here;
If heaven's by works, in heaven they can't appear;
Ah, reason, how depraved!
Revere the sacred page, the knot's untied;
They died, for Adam sinned; they live, for Jesus died."

The second argument from Paul's language arises from the fact that he attributes the condemnation of the human race to the one offence of Adam. It is perfectly clear from his statements that we are not held liable for any of the sins of Adam, except the eating of the forbidden fruit; and for that one offence death has passed upon the race. It is just as plain, if this is so, that we are not connected with Adam simply as children are connected with a parent. A father may commit many errors and his children may suffer repeatedly through him. He may commit errors in his business, and his heirs may suffer for every loss he meets. He may believe mischievous doctrines, and every one may be transmitted for evil to his posterity. He may contract diseases, and these may become hereditary. The merely natural connection between a parent and a child, gives the parent power analogous to that of a representative, but it is not limited to one offence. But in the case of Adam our whole responsibility does turn upon one offence; and that is just such a one as might be committed by a parent without bringing special mischief on his posterity. This limitation to one offence, and these great effects flowing from one, can be explained only by believing that we stood in Adam—that we fell in Adam, when he partook of the forbidden tree, in a sense that is not true of any of Adam's personal obligations or personal transgressions.

When God called, "Adam, where art thou?" and the reply was a falsehood, nothing is said of laying that offence upon us. Adam, doubtless, committed other sins in nine hundred years; but by his *one offence* death reigns. He was our natural head through all his life; he was our federal head in regard to that one thing; for the covenant demanded obedience respecting the fruit of the tree.

Without attempting to express any further reasons to prove the fact that a covenant was made with Adam, except the clear proof which arises from Paul's parallel between Adam and Christ, which we reserve for other chapters, it may be proper to advert to the practical influence of the doctrine thus advocated as corroborative of its truth. No intelligent man can question the intellectual vigour and the warm-hearted piety of the men who have held these views; no one can doubt that they can use in expressing their views the impressive language of the Bible upon the subject of man's sin; and it is equally beyond question that these teachings are most decidedly rejected by ungodly and wicked men, who have no serious thoughts concerning any of their sins, and no true reverence for God at all. No doubt many a Christian can remember when he quarrelled with the doctrine of man's native depravity, or perhaps found in it excuses for carelessness. But let a man lay aside his pride; let him look at the well known facts of his sins and of God's justice; let him justify God's holy law and holy character, even in things he does not understand; and he will find these teachings, never pleasant, but deeply humbling and profitable.

When a man justifies God in all his doings as David did, and yet confesses with David that he was "conceived and born in sin;" when he recognizes that he has been a sinner from the very beginning of his life, he may well abhor himself for his vileness and pray fervently, "Create in me a clean heart, O God." I may not find fault with the Lord; nor say to my Maker, Why hast thou made me thus? But with a sinful nature, I ought to be humble; with such depraved tendencies, I need to watch against temptation and sin; and the more I know of my sinful, and wretched, and lost estate, the more thankful I ought to be that God has not left our race to perish in guilt; that he has provided a mighty Redeemer, and that he calls me to wash away the stain of numerous offences in the fountain of atoning blood.

CHAPTER XXIII.

ADAM—THE FIRST AND THE SECOND.

"The Second Adam from the dust
Raises the ruins of the First."

WATTS.

THERE is no historical question of surpassing interest to a serious Christian, beyond that which would inquire into the early knowledge of the human family concerning redemption. It is not only true that the sacred Scriptures place the sin of man and the mercy of God in constant contiguity; urging man's utter ruin as the great reason why he should seek the Divine method of recovery; but God's mercy was taught to the first sinners even before they gave any tokens of ingenuous sorrow. How much was known of the gospel in the first days of its proclamation? When we read that our first parents were clothed in skins of God's providing, instead of the scanty fig-leaf aprons they had themselves prepared, are we to understand that these were the skins of beasts slain in the Paradise they had just defiled—slain as sacrificial offerings to atone for the guilt they had just contracted—slain as prophetic and sacramental symbols of that coming Redeemer, whose conflict with Satan, whose bruising and whose triumph had just been foretold? When we read of Abel's bleeding sacrifice as a custom already established and sufficiently understood; when his faith and Cain's unbelief clearly imply Divine teachings to which both should have conformed; and when man's need of the gospel and God's grace in the gospel seem in the Scriptures to belong to every age of human history; are we from all these things to conclude that Adam knew Christ and the way of salvation through the blood of atonement? There can be little doubt about the most important matters involved in such an investigation. Adam knew the way of salvation as truly as any of his children since. He knew he was a sinner beyond a doubt; and he knew that God proclaimed mercy to the repenting sinner.

Mark! We say he knew as *truly;* we do not say he knew as *clearly* and *plainly.* The facts before his mind were less numerous; the teachings less explicit; and it is difficult to decide how well he knew the great principles of the Divine procedure. But the gospel was then the same that it is now; God has ever saved guilty men through the death of his Son; the sacrifices instituted in the days of Adam, were designed to prefigure the sufferings of Christ; and the Apostle Paul teaches us that Adam himself stood in a remarkable relation to Christ; that he was himself a *figure*, or, to use the original word, a *type* of him that was to come.

Adam is expressly called a type of Christ. Surely the language contains important and profitable teaching. And this teaching should possess double interest, because we learn from it both the relation sustained to his children by Adam, and the relation sustained to his people by Christ. The covenant made with Christ as the Mediator between God and man is clearly revealed in the sacred writings; but, from the evident meaning of Paul, Adam sustained a like relation, and was alike bound by a covenant. So that we establish the fact that a covenant was made with Adam for his race, while we learn of the covenant made of God in Christ.

We should not desire to separate these teachings. Distinct as the topics are; much as the angels in heaven know of sin, though they have never tasted sin; much as the devils in hell know of salvation, though they shall never be saved; let sinful man—a prisoner of hope—learn the two lessons together. While he knows of his nature fallen through the first Adam, let him know that the Redeemer of the fallen bears the name of the Second Adam; and let him understand that the largest acquaintance with our ruined condition through the *type* in Paradise, should produce, not rebellion and despair, but repentance and love through the *Antitype* of Calvary.

It is well worthy of our notice that Paul's entire description of Adam and of the relation borne by him to the race in the covenant of works, is incidental. He speaks with the air of a man giving instructions with which his hearers are already familiar. We have no such explanations as usually accompany new lessons; he takes it for granted that the readers of the epistle to the Romans are already well acquainted with the facts and principles here mentioned; and the very use he makes of them is proof that he did not consider his words as conveying doctrines either new or strange. His introduction of Adam is solely to illustrate a different matter. This is apparent. *As* this, *so* that, are terms used by those who would illustrate. But in the very nature of human language, and in the necessities of rhetoric, illustrations can properly be drawn only from things already understood. Illustrations to a discourse are like windows to a house. They are designed to let in the light; and they serve this purpose best, when they are themselves transparent. Paul takes it for granted that his views concerning Adam were already well understood in the Church of God; and though we may not be able to tell when they were first so clearly known, yet his sentiments seem only the more forcible from this manner of uttering them. They are too plain and too well known to need any argument; too easily understood to need explanation.

The apostle expressly tells us that Adam was a figure or type of Him that was to come. In another epistle he again compares them; declares that as death came by Adam, so life comes by Christ; and calls the one the first and the other the last Adam. Even the name of Adam is thus applied to Christ; there must be then a remarkable likeness between them. They are not in all points alike. The one is earthly, the other heavenly; the second is every way superior to the first; yet ought we carefully to consider both the points of analogy and the points of difference.

Adam was a type of Christ,

First, because he stood as a public person and in a representative capacity, when he ate the fruit of the forbidden tree.

Our reasoning may be the reverse of Paul's, for our object is opposite. His design is to illustrate salvation and the means by which it becomes ours, by the fall and the means by which we are involved in it. He explains Christ by Adam. We design rather to explain Adam by Christ; the covenant of works by the covenant of grace; the fall and the things implied in it, by the gospel and its methods. Paul's facts and principles exactly suit our purpose; and we hope to reach the same end with Paul, reasoning from his conclusions to his premises.

That Christ was our representative and suffered not in a private but a public capacity, no Christian man can doubt. No private reasons urged the Son of the Eternal to become incarnate; no personal sinfulness brought upon him the sufferings he bore;

and the blessings secured by him were for his free bestowal upon others. He is the Surety of a covenant; he laid down his life for others, and great as are the mysteries of Christ's redeeming love, the mystery of his character and object, of his griefs and his success, is incomparably greater; indeed is entirely inexplicable, unless we receive this simplest of all truths—that Christ Jesus was a public person in all his earthly work.

But if we cannot otherwise understand the position and influence of Christ than as he was a public person, neither can we understand the influence of Adam or the comparison made between the two, except by believing the same thing. The language of Paul is easily understood, if we acknowledge the public and representative capacity of Adam; it is impossible to see why he speaks of him at all, and how we can explain the facts he states, except as we do receive this. He declares that sin entered by one man's one offence; and death comes by sin. He anticipates the objection that a large number of our race die who have never sinned, by teaching that this death can only be accounted for by this very truth, that Adam was a type of Christ in this, that he was a public person. His concise argument is, "Wherever there is death there is sin; wherever there is sin there is law; wherever death comes, it comes as the penalty of law, and is, therefore, the proof of a law violated; wherever such a penalty comes upon those who have not personally violated the law, they must have broken it by the act of another: and this necessarily implies the doctrine of representation." If death passed upon all men for that all sinned; if yet this sentence of condemnation is for the offence of one; if the disobedience of a single one makes many sinners; if death reigns universally, not because of universal sinfulness, but because of that one original offence,—these all are terms utterly void of meaning, unless Adam was under a covenant, a public and representative person.

CHAPTER XXIV.

THE AFFILIATED DOCTRINES.

ADAM was a type of Christ,

Secondly, Because the principles that are involved in the gospel of Christ are implied in man's fall in Adam, and the reception of salvation by Christ requires that in consistency we should acknowledge our union in Adam.

We say the principles are the same; but the application, we shall see, is for opposite purposes. "As in Adam all die, so in Christ shall all be made alive."

1. We need but mention, without further repetition, that the doctrine of Representation belongs both to Christ and to Adam; both were public persons; and if we can see that one could stand in this relation, no righteous principle forbids that the other should. The entire doctrine of atonement by Christ rests upon his public and representative character.

2. The doctrine of Imputation as clearly belongs to the true teachings concerning both Adam and Christ.

Nothing can be more explicit than the negative and the positive teachings of the Bible concerning the sufferings of Christ. On the one hand, it is denied that he suffered for his own sins; for he knew no sin, was holy, harmless, undefiled, and separate from sinners; and on the other hand, it is affirmed that he did suffer for the sins of others, for he bore our sins in his own body on the tree, he was bruised for our iniquities, he was a ransom for us. We say then in view of these statements that our sins were imputed to Christ; by which we do not mean that Christ became a sinner, for we expressly affirm that he was spotless; nor that our characteristics were transferred to him; nor that he must feel, or could feel, the remorse which our sins may awaken in us; but simply that he became legally liable to suffer the penalty of the broken law for us. Liability to suffer for us is the true meaning of the term when we affirm that our sins were imputed to Christ; and this is the only consistent meaning of many passages of sacred teaching: "Christ also hath suffered for us, the Just for the unjust;" "He hath made him to be sin for us;" "He hath borne our iniquity."

But the doctrine of imputation belongs, in another most important sense, to the Scriptural teachings concerning Christ. It is by the imputation of the righteousness of Christ that believers are justified before God. In vain would he bear our sins if we were not justified by his righteousness. These things belong necessarily together. If, as the Surety of his people, Christ is held liable for the judgment against them, his satisfaction of the judgment is their release. If God has made him, who knew no sin, to be sin for us, it is that we, who knew no righteousness, should be made the righteousness of God in him. Very plainly do the Scriptures deny that any sinner can be justified before God by his own works; and as plainly do they teach that the righteousness of Christ received by faith is the sole ground of a sinner's acceptance.

But the doctrine of imputation, thus taught respecting Christ, is taught also respecting Adam. True of Christ in two respects, it is true of Adam in one respect. As our covenant head, Christ suffers for us, and we receive the benefit of his public acts. As our covenant head, we fell in Adam. Look at Paul's contrasted words through all this passage. Rom. v. 12—21. Law is by Adam, grace is by Christ; death is by Adam, life is by Christ; condemnation by Adam, justification by Christ; disobedience by Adam, obedience by Christ; sin is by Adam, righteousness is by Christ; the only exception, as we shall hereafter see, arises from the superiority of the second Adam in all he is and was.

Nor should we omit to say that while the doctrine of imputation is thus essentially involved in both the covenants, of which Christ and Adam are the Federal Heads respectively, the usual cavillings of men against the doctrine as urged in regard to

Adam may be answered most clearly by just thoughts of imputation in regard to Christ. And every ingenuous mind may find a reply to its own chief difficulties by carefully noticing these analogies.

Is it objected that Adam's sin must be his own and cannot be ours; and that every man must suffer for his own sins? Make the objection true and consistent; and salvation is impossible to man. Unless Christ suffered for sins that were not personally his own, we never can be saved. Is it objected that character cannot be transferred? We reply that, as before declared, this is not the proper meaning of imputation. It refers to legal responsibility; and in this sense the analogy holds between Christ and Adam. Paul's words are of equal force in the two directions: "As by one man's disobedience many were made sinners, so by the obedience of one shall many be made righteous." Is it objected that we cannot feel remorse for the sin of Adam in which we are condemned? It is an exact reply to say, neither can we feel any self complacency for the righteousness of Christ by which we are justified. Yet we may feel humbled that we are fallen in Adam; and we may feel grateful that we rise in Christ.

3. To affirm the existence of the covenant of works with Adam as our head in it, and the covenant of grace with Christ as our head in it, alone can explain these preceding doctrines, and

the facts as we are taught them by the word and providence of God.

All that we are able to learn of Christ may be made to illustrate what we would know of Adam; and all we know of Adam may illustrate the truth respecting Christ. For, in Paul's teachings, the correspondence between them is almost entirely exact. There are differences as we shall see. But in the chief principle of their respective positions, that a covenant was made with both, they are as alike as possible. The method of man's ruin corresponds to the method of his recovery. In both cases it is through another. In Adam, our natural father, his children stood in Eden. Adam sinned. We thus became sinners, are under condemnation, and suffer death. In Christ, our spiritual Head, his people stood. He satisfied the broken law. We are made righteous by one man's obedience; his righteousness is the ground of our justification; we partake of eternal life through him. All is clear if we believe the doctrines of the two covenants, of vicarious substitution, of representation, and imputation; but we have no key to unlock these intricate mysteries, if these things are not true both of the first and the second Adam.

CHAPTER XXV.

THE SECOND ADAM GREATER.

"Where sin did reign and death abound,
There have the sons of Adam found
Abounding life; there glorious grace
Reigns through the LORD OUR RIGHTEOUSNESS."
WATTS.

BUT, thirdly, the parallel between Adam and Christ is not complete. We ought to bring clearly into view the great and precious truth that Christ is greater than Adam. The apostle gives us occasion for devout thanksgiving when he declares, that the sin and the gift are not alike; for "where sin abounded, grace did much more abound."

The points of superiority are such as these:

1. Condemnation is by law and justice; salvation is by gift and grace. We have no just ideas upon these topics, unless we acknowledge the entire righteousness of God in man's condemnation, and recognize his sovereignty and grace in our recovery. But how glorious is the conception of grace to those who are condemned by a law so holy! So excellent is this, that the Scriptures speak of God himself

glorying in it; and commending his love for sinners, as he commends no other of the Divine acts. There was nothing to excite the wonder of adoring angels when God executed his wrath upon Satan and his hosts; but to see the exercise of love and grace, and especially by methods so wonderful as the death of his own Son, towards rebellious men, might well affect them with the greatest surprise and admiration. Nor do we have just views of Christ's coming to save, except when we refer it to the sovereign, unmerited grace of God, wonderful alike as shown in his Son and to the rebellious.

2. Recovery is always more difficult than ruin; to destroy is always more easy than to repair. One fatal sin brought wretchedness upon our race, as a spark may kindle a conflagration in whose fiery path innumerable palaces and countless stores of wealth may be reduced to ashes. But not so easy was the task of the Redeemer; and it is to the glory of Christ, that he shrank not back from the work of man's salvation, although even by him it was not easily accomplished.

3. The apostle makes a distinct point of contrast in the facts that by one sin of Adam the race is ruined; but that by Christ's work his people are redeemed, not only from that one offence, but also from their own numerous and aggravated offences. If it is amazing grace that forgives a single sin, how may we magnify the mercy of God in Christ by which the manifold iniquities of a man, the mul-

tiplied transgressions of so many men, the aggravated guilt of the chief of sinners, are so freely forgiven!

4. Christ is superior to Adam, for the effect of His grace upon every believer does much more than restore him to the estate from which Adam fell.

What man has lost in the fall of Adam is much less than what is gained by the redemption of Christ. Not only is the enmity of sinful minds taken away in Christ; not only the image of God restored to the soul; not only the darkened mind enlightened; the perverted will renewed; the defiled conscience purified; and the grovelling affections elevated. We are not placed by Christ in a new state of probation, in which our righteousness is to secure for us the favour of our God. Salvation by Christ is not only by grace, upon terms wholly different from man's original standing under the covenant of works, but it places us in a more glorious estate. Adam was liable to fall; Christ's people can never perish. Though Adam and his race had the prospect of eternal life, they never secured it; but the people of Christ shall surely enter upon the possession of everlasting peace.

5. Christ Jesus, as the Second Adam, is superior to Adam the first, because of his unquestionable and infallible accomplishment of the great work he has undertaken for the salvation of his people.

How excellent was the object of the first covenant, had our first father stood in Paradise! how disastrous was his fall! Can we entertain the fear that like disaster, or even failure, at any point, or for any child of the covenant, is possible to Him whom now we are called to trust? Here is a most important point of Christ's superiority, that his work cannot possibly fail. Well may our Mediator be called the SURETY of a better covenant; for his redeemed people none can pluck out of his hand.

We might argue this conclusion from the infinite perfections of the Divine character; from the excellency of our glorious Redeemer; from the very nature of the covenant made of God in Christ; from the express teachings of the Scriptures; and from the superior security thus afforded to the people of Christ.

The great work of God for his own glory is not one of doubtful accomplishment. The All-knowing, the Almighty has not undertaken what he cannot do; nor promised to the Son what he cannot fulfil. That must be a false view of the scheme of redemption which represents God as defeated, or the Son of God as disappointed in the results. It is strange, indeed, if Christ suffers in a public capacity, fulfils all the terms demanded of him as a Surety, and yet receives not in full the promised reward. The Father doeth his pleasure; the promises of God are sure; the Son shall see of the travail of his soul and shall be satisfied. Christ's words are explicit. "All that the Father giveth me shall come to me, and him that cometh unto me I will in no wise cast out."

We understand that the covenant of grace was made with Christ for his chosen people, for his spiritual seed, and that every soul interested in it shall receive the reward of His work. As the former covenant was for Adam's natural seed, so the second covenant is for Christ's spiritual seed. So Christ lays down his life for his sheep; so he laid hold, not on the seed of Adam, but on the seed of Abraham; so he made with David "an everlasting covenant ordered in all things and sure," 2 Sam. xxiii. 5; so he promises to every repenting soul to make with him "an everlasting covenant, even the sure mercies of David," Isa. lv. 3. We do not understand that the covenant made with Christ includes the entire race of man, in the same sense that this is true of the covenant made with Adam. This cannot be true, unless we receive the doctrine of universal salvation; and even this upon grounds entirely different from the usual advocacy of its modern defenders. A dogma contradicted so expressly by the Bible, and by the entire scope of its teachings, cannot form part of our faith. We cannot believe that Christ died for the men who perished in the flood, just as for Noah who was saved in the ark; for the Sodomites, as for Abraham who vainly prayed that God would spare them; for the presumptuous king who perished in the Red Sea, and for the believing prophet who led Israel through dry-shod. All these had already passed from earth before Christ died; and we cannot believe that he had any design to save those who had already perished. In reference to all the past and all the future of the human family, the designs of the Redemeer for salvation are entirely like the accomplishment of them; and he cannot fail to complete the entire work he has undertaken.

We do not pretend to explain why God has not made salvation universal for the human family. We must content ourselves with believing what he has revealed in his word and providence; and it is ours to believe that reasons of infinite wisdom and rectitude govern all he does. We are well aware that many perplexities attend a careful investigation of topics like these. Yet we believe that fewer difficulties gather around the truth as thus held, than around any other explanation of the covenant of grace; while there are special advantages belonging to these views. If there is a covenant, that covenant ought to be carried out. Did Christ undertake what he could not perform? or the Father promise what he will not fulfil? May one man be truly bought by the precious blood of Christ, and yet perish for ever? What then is the assurance to any other man, that he may not also perish? The chief encouragement that ought to lead any man to trust Christ is this great fact, that no soul interested in this everlasting covenant can perish. We may well trust the salvation of our souls to such a Redeemer. Well might Paul say, "I know whom I have believed, and am persuaded that he is able to keep that which I have committed unto him against that day." 2 Tim. i. 12.

Many persons are perplexed with some aspects of this matter. Especially they say, How can God offer salvation to every creature that hears the gospel? or how can I trust to Christ unless I know that he has died for me? But the same difficulty in regard to the Divine sincerity must arise from God's foreknowledge upon any view of the atonement; and it is never true that our duties depend upon a previous acquaintance with the purposes of God. The chief difficulty upon the entire subject of salvation, as presented in the Scriptures, arises from the fact that men perplex themselves to discover how God and man can both be free. It arises from God's infinite perfection, that all his plans are complete and unchangeable; how this can be, when he deals with sinful and fallible men, we cannot comprehend. Yet these facts we may know: God is sovereign and immutable, and man is free and accountable. How this is so, we presume not to explain; but no reasonable man can gainsay the facts.

If the question be asked, Upon what grounds may a sinner come to Christ and hope for salvation through his atonement, when he does not know that he is among the number of those given to Christ by the Father? we need not go far to find an answer.

We have better hopes of a sure salvation, and we have the same assurance of our acceptance, that we could have upon any other view of the work of Christ. Let any man consider upon any view of the atonement, what is the true reason to hope that God will receive us. Is it not the PROMISE OF GOD? He pledgeth himself that whosoever believeth shall be saved. We do not need to read his secret counsels in order to learn our duties or our privileges. We know from what he has said, that every believer shall be saved; indeed we have his oath and his promise, "that by two immutable things in which it is impossible for God to lie, we might have strong consolation who have fled to lay hold on the hope set before us in the gospel." Heb. vi. 18. And these two great things—the redemption of a chosen people, and the gracious assurance of acceptance to every humble sinner, are by our Lord directly connected with each other. "All that the Father giveth me, shall come to me, and him that cometh unto me I will in no wise cast out." John vi. 37.

This is the excellence of the work of Christ, that it shall certainly and fully be accomplished. The first Adam failed, the second Adam cannot. Surely this ought to be a reason of the most urgent nature, to lead every sinful soul to seek an interest in this great salvation. And the various perplexities that spring up, and which multiply because neither our ignorance nor our depravity will allow us to see things as God sees them, yet should not be allowed to cloud the plain teachings of the Bible, or to hinder our acceptance of its precious promises. Let us seriously ask counsel of God in regard to some of our perplexities, refer others absolutely to his will; and find in all of them, reasons for devout thanksgiving that the most needful teachings are the plainest.

These are plain truths, that we are guilty and lost sinners; that we have sinned much, and long, and wilfully; and that we must perish if we are not renewed by the Holy Spirit, and interested in the precious blood of Christ. And these are truths as plain, that Christ is able to save; that his blood is efficacious to purge the vilest; that he proclaims salvation in our ears, invites every sinner to come, and promises that for no reason in the world will he cast out any one who does come. Both these classes of truths are as plain as the word of God can make them. Let any one read the fifty-fifth chapter of Isaiah, and decide if any larger or freer terms could be offered to men. "Ho, every one! come without money," come with perplexity, come with sin, come with fear; but COME. "Incline your ear and come unto me; hear, and your souls shall live; and I will make an everlasting covenant with you, even the sure mercies of David." It cannot be expected that we can know all the depths of mercy in this gracious God, for he adds by the prophet this express assurance, "My thoughts are not your thoughts, neither are your ways my ways, saith the Lord."

Happy is the man who joins his soul to God in Christ in the bonds of this "everlasting covenant ordered in all things and sure." It has no excellency superior to this, that it cannot fail; and Christ Jesus has no glory greater than this, that he is able and willing to save to the uttermost all that come unto God by him. No man can defeat the Divine purposes, or defraud the Redeemer of his reward. Sinful men can refuse the mercy of God to their own just condemnation. But whosoever accepts the Divine offers, and joins himself to God in this covenant, shall certainly be saved. How gladly should men say to each other, as they ask the way to Zion and have their faces thitherward, "Come and let us join ourselves to the Lord, in a perpetual covenant that shall not be forgotten!" Jer. l. 5.

CHAPTER XXVI.

ADAM'S FIRST BORN SONS.

FROM these thoughts upon the union of our race in our first father, it is proper now to pass on to the subsequent events in his history.

It is likely that the mercy of God, mingled with the sentence pronounced upon them, and especially the promise of a coming Redeemer, led our first parents to the exercise of a genuine repentance. The plan of salvation, at least so far as it is taught in the solemn offering of typical sacrifices, was doubtless explained to them; and their faith was directed towards atoning blood, and yet taught to look forward to the coming Sufferer. We can hardly think that principles and services so significant would be so abruptly begun among men, with no special design, and with no understanding of their meaning. We find these things introduced into the history as abruptly as possible. Adam and Eve were clothed in skins; and we are not told whence the skins were derived. But as animal food was not then eaten, it is natural to conclude that the beasts were slain in sacrifice.

We find Abel offering a sacrifice and accepted by faith; but the language seems to imply that he here fulfils duties already familiar to man. We conclude from these things, that God gave Adam directions for his worship, such as suited a sinner; and we hope, rather than know, that our first parents repented of their sins, worshipped God acceptably according to his directions, and found forgiveness through atoning blood. We cannot judge that they clearly knew the things revealed to us; but we are to recognize that God's method of saving sinners was the same then as now.

But the forgiveness of a penitent according to God's method of mercy, is not the same as an immediate restoration to an estate of innocence. Even forgiven Adam must go forth from Paradise, and be debarred access to the tree of life. As we see now in the experience of the church that regenerated souls are not souls made perfect in holiness; as God designs to fit his people for his service, not by completing at once and without various means, the work of making them like himself; as long conflict with temptation, and many checkered scenes make up the life of the true believer, so our first parents must go forth from their pleasant home, and submit to the evils their folly and sin had introduced. The free forgiveness of sin according to the gospel of Christ, does not stay the natural results of sin already committed, nor defeat the workings of God's well ordered laws.

We may well suppose that Adam and Eve were deeply grieved and humbled by their expulsion from the garden. We can easily adopt as the lamentation of Eve the familiar lines of Milton :—

> " Must I leave thee, Paradise? Thus leave
> Thee, native soil, these happy walks and shades,
> Fit haunt of gods? where I had hoped to spend,
> Quiet though sad, the respite of that day
> That must be mortal to us both . . . . .
> . . . How shall we breathe in other air
> Less pure, accustomed to immortal fruits?"

Nor less was that a proof of their fallen estate that an angel and a flaming sword should guard the gate, and should forbid them to approach the Tree of Life.

The incidents recorded in the long lives of Adam and Eve are few; and the names of but a few of their children are given. As the human race attained to extraordinary age in these early times, we cannot decide certainly whether the adult period was reached in twenty years as now, or whether it came later. Yet we know that this period came then earlier than to us in proportion to the length of life. Their years were tenfold ours; but their adult period was not two hundred as compared with our twenty. We read of fathers at sixty-five, seventy, and ninety; and it may be true, that the childhood of the Antediluvians was no longer than the childhood that belongs to our briefer term of life. It is very easy to show, upon any reasonable supposition, that the advance in population must have been rapid. Within a few hundred years from the creation, many thousands of men lived upon the earth.

The first-born in the family of Adam was named Cain. We can easily imagine that it was an hour of joy in the earth when this child was born. The love of a mother for her first-born is proverbial. A new affection is then also born; and it comes with a vigour and freshness that fills the mind with delight as she gazes upon the helpless being entrusted to her care. But how strong was this affection in Eve as she looked upon the first of first-born! and her rejoicing at his birth was greater, if she mistook him—as it is generally thought—for the promised seed. The name Cain signifies possession; for said she, "I have gotten a man, the Lord."

Alas! how wonderfully may the fond hopes of a mother be disappointed. She looks with affection upon her infant boy; she shields him from all evil which a mother's care can ward off; she tenderly cares for his helplessness, and supplies his wants; but he will soon go forth to scenes over which a mother cannot watch; to dangers from which a mother cannot protect; and to sins that may change a mother's early joy to the deepest grief. What a contrast between Eve's hopes when she thought that her first-born would avenge her quarrel with the serpent, and the sad reality in the subsequent history of Cain! The responsibility of a parent's care should always chasten

19*

the joy with which we look upon our beloved children, and the hopes we entertain of what they are to be. And doubtless we would have wiser parents and happier children, if both could better realize how much their usefulness and happiness are mutually dependent. A parent may do much to form the child for future good or evil; and the misconduct of a child may bring grief and sorrow upon an aged parent.

There was a great difference in character between the two eldest sons of Adam, whose names are given us. Something of this may be traced to a great difference in natural disposition, and perhaps healthfulness. The different occupations of the two may give us a hint of this. Cain was a tiller of the ground. Doubtless the arts of agriculture were rude at first; as even to this day, a very imperfect system of tillage prevails in all the lands of the Bible. And in that early age, the earth may have felt so little the influence of the curse; thorns had spread so little abroad, and land was so abundant, that the tiller's occupation may not have exacted so severe labour as now. Still, the toil of cultivating the earth was greater than was required for a shepherd's life. Adam trained both for industry. But the name Abel signifies *vanity*. It is not uncommon in the East to change the name after any important event. This name seems so significant of his early removal from earth, that we are almost led to judge that it was given after his death, or that it was dictated by a prophetic spirit.

Yet the name may indicate a weak and feeble constitution. And that he possessed such, may be the reason for assigning to him the lighter duties of a shepherd. But the engagements of the brothers were alike useful and honourable. Few engagements afford better opportunities for self-culture and improvement than both of these. In both there are advantages for solitary thought; occasions to notice the providences of God, and much dependence upon the Divine blessing for success. A nation is prosperous where these two earliest occupations of men prosper; and corruption of morals and manners is less likely to prevail where either the pastoral or the agricultural interest is chiefly promoted.

We judge that, of course, Adam taught his sons the principles and duties of religion, and trained them to the acts of worship enjoined upon him. Yet we gather what these were only from the narrative. It is one of the characteristics of the Bible that some of our most important religious services are spoken of familiarly with no account of their origin. In the New Testament, baptism, first with John in the wilderness, and afterwards by Christ and his disciples, is spoken of as a religious service; of whose origin we have no account, and whose design we gather from various teachings. So in the Old Testament when we first meet with sacrifice, it is already an established rite; no account is given of its institution, and its design is learned from far later teachings.

We are told that the sons of Adam both worshipped God. "In process of time," it is said, they brought their offerings. The margin reads, "at the end of days." It seems to be at an appointed time, and may mean, as some interpreters understand it, upon the Sabbath-day. We cannot suppose, of course, that Adam taught his sons different methods of worship; yet we find them offering diverse things, and their acceptance was not alike before God. Alas! this fruit of sin was not wanting in the very family of Adam, that so early in the history of the race, perverse worship is offered to God, and the simple faith of the gospel is despised by man's proud powers of reason.

CHAPTER XXVII.

THE WORSHIP OF CAIN.

We are suddenly introduced in the inspired narrative to the first recorded acts of human worship: with no immediate explanation of the meaning of these things, we have no assigned cause for the rejection of one worshipper and the acceptance of the other. Yet we are not to judge from the silence of the inspired pages, that these two brothers who stand before the same God, had received no instructions as to God's requirements for acceptable service. They knew how to approach him; and as the principles of appropriate worship were the same then as in later times, we also may know the nature of their offerings, and the reasons of God's diverse dealings with them.

We see these brothers approach God with different offerings. If we judge according to the principles of human reasonings, we may be disposed to conclude that both their offerings are such as we might expect them to bring. When a man brings the best he has to God; when he offers the fruit of his own toil; when he acknowledges his subjection to Divine authority, and his dependence upon the Divine will, would we not suppose that he would be accepted? Cain was a cultivator of the earth, and it seemed suitable that he should bring the things which sprung up from the earth through his toil. Abel was a keeper of sheep, and the increase of his flock seemed a fitting offering on his part. The Almighty indeed did not need any offering from either of them. But it was by his blessing that their labours had proved productive; and these, his dependent creatures, ought thankfully to acknowledge his care. It seems reasonable that each should bring what has come of his own toils.

But we will make a great mistake if we reason in this way, and leave out of view that these were not simply God's creatures coming to worship their Creator; but that they were sinful beings approaching that God whose mercy they should implore. The offering that might be becoming in a holy being might be insulting, should a sinner presume to approach, as if there was nothing between him and his God. It would seem from the narrative that Cain was no atheist; he recognized a God; recognized the true God; recognized his dependence upon God; was willing to express his gratitude to God; but he did not come as a sinner, and no part of his offering gave any token of penitence. If even we believe, though it is not expressly said, that Cain brought of the first fruits and of the chief fruits of his labours, still this was no acceptable offering from a sinner. The covenant of works was broken; man's best deeds were already defiled; Cain cannot find God's favour thus.

The offering of Abel was different in its nature. He offered a lamb; but he offered its blood. The sacrifice of the altar was the method of acceptable approach to God.

It is surely a remarkable thing that the offering of bleeding sacrifices should be so universal among men. And we can give no reasonable account of such a service, unless we receive the teachings of the sacred Scriptures, and learn here the important principles which belong to this method of worship. We shall speak in a subsequent chapter of Abel and his offering, and then attempt to unfold more clearly the signification of this rite. Suffice it here to say, that as prophecy in Eden had already declared the coming of the Woman's Seed, the great Deliverer and Redeemer of fallen man; so sacrifice was instituted to typify him as the Lamb of God, who should bleed and die to take away the sin of the world. So far as we are concerned, the chief explanations of this were given long afterwards; but it is likely that the first worshippers were taught something of the meaning of this solemn rite. Indeed, mysterious as it is in some of its aspects, the service explained itself before the eyes of all who offered it. How could any man confess his sins solemnly over the head of a living animal, pour out its blood at the foot of the rude altar, offer it then in the burning flame, and know that all this was by the command of God, without understanding that by this service must be set forth some significance of the forgiveness of sin?

We are told that Abel offered his sacrifice in faith; and the implication is that Cain's offering was one of unbelief. Yet very plainly it was not unbelief in God's existence; nor was it an entire refusal to recognize his claims. Had Cain felt thus, he would have brought nothing. Cain worshipped God according to his own pleasure, and not according to the Divine direction. Religion for a sinner is a matter of revelation, not of reason; and thus early in the history of the world the line of distinction between these two things is clearly drawn. Of course we do not mean that revelation is unreasonable; the very reverse is true. Nothing is more reasonable than that God himself should instruct ignorant and sinful man; and it is the unreasonableness of pride and sin which makes man refuse to hear. We ought to judge that so great a thing as the restoration of sinners to the favour of a holy God, would surpass the wisdom of man, and could only be learned through Divine teachings. It is important for us to know that the spirit which actuated the first errorist is yet alive upon earth, and even dwells in the hearts of many who wish not to compare themselves with the first murderer. Cain had not indeed gone so far as to refuse all worship to God; but to worship by halves is a step in the direction of not worshipping at all. But how many men there are, who ought to be better instructed, who think that all that God requires of them is the honest, and upright, and industrious discharge of their duties in society, some respect for his name, and some recognition of their dependence upon him? They see no necessity for that kind of religion that weeps for sin at the foot of the cross of Christ; that sits in penitence around the sacramental board; and that feels a deep anxiety for the salvation of other men. We say nothing now of the history of Cain after this first offering; but so far as this first-born of Eve is here brought before us, is not his religion just such a religion as this? He was an honest, industrious labourer in the fields; he drew near to God with at least some measure of respect; he knew that his daily bread was the gift of a bountiful Providence.

We are expressly taught in the New Testament that no man can find God's favour by any works of righteousness done by himself, at any time, or for any purpose. This is not only because our best works are imperfect and defiled; but because we are sinners and must be reconciled to God by the blood of atonement. There are only two ways possible by which God's creatures can please him: one is by a perfect righteousness of their own, which sinners cannot possibly show before his holy sight; and the other is by the atonement of Christ. Both these methods are here exhibited in these two sons of Adam. Abel is accepted because he believed God, and offered blood before him to signify the death of the coming Redeemer; and Cain was rejected because he brought no such offering as this. And every man will be rejected now, who has folly and daring enough to follow in the footsteps of Cain. Let any man think that his own reason is enough to guide him, while he rejects God's express teachings in the Bible; let any man suppose that his own works are enough to secure God's favour, and that if one but discharges his usual duties in society, he has no special need for dependence upon the blood of Christ; let any man judge that if he attends upon the house of God, is respectful towards religion, and grateful for the mercies of Providence, he need not fear. Yet such men are not believers in the footsteps of Abel; and they may well hear the solemn warning of the Apostle Jude, "Wo unto them, for they have gone in the way of Cain!"

CHAPTER XXVIII.

THE REJECTION OF CAIN.

We are not told by what means Cain and Abel knew immediately the results of their worship. Perhaps there was an appointed spot where God was pleased specially to dwell; and there were well known means by which his favour was indicated. Long afterwards upon several occasions, fire descended from God to consume the sacrifices made to him; and thus he may have answered the altar of Abel.

Cain knew that he was rejected; and it filled him with rage. This itself is a proof that he did not approach God with an humble and penitent mind, as became a sinner. It is not needful that we should even attempt to discover the thoughts of Cain towards God. If even we could analyze the feelings of the first unbeliever; if we could know what he said and why he rebelled, it would be unprofitable knowledge. The humble heart knows enough of the workings of sin within itself to cause it to mourn before God; and the proud heart is too fruitful in evil to need any lessons such as Cain could teach. But we know well that renewed pride and rage against God, was never the fruit of right feelings in any man. True penitence would have cast Cain down before God with grief at the sign of rejection; and if he had felt as he should, he could have entertained no hard feelings towards Abel. For he surely was not the cause of his brother's rejection.

In striking and affecting contrast with the anger of Cain is the long suffering mercy of God. We may see here the plain difference between the Divine favour and the Divine forbearance. God did not accept the offering of Cain, nor smile upon him as a worshipper; but neither did he, in just displeasure for his renewed iniquity, turn utterly away from the unbeliever. As it is in our times according to the teachings of Christ's Apostles, that God's goodness, and forbearance, and long-suffering, are designed and adapted to lead men to repentance and salvation, (Rom. ii. 4; 2 Pet. iii. 15,) so was it in the days of God's earliest mercy. God expostulated with him; he pointed out to him the unreasonableness of his anger; and he laid the blame of the rejection at the sinner's own door. Perhaps the direction for Cain's proper acceptance refers not so much to his natural duty of obedience to the moral law, as to his duty to comply with the divinely appointed methods of worship. "If thou doest well, shalt thou not be accepted? and if thou doest not well, sin lieth at the door."

If even we suppose the words refer to any duties of the creature, God is justified in his dealings with the sinner. His displeasure is of justice, and arises from man's sin; and we are specially sinful, if we neither satisfy his justice nor seek his mercy. He that doeth well shall be accepted; and every sinner may find the means of approaching for acceptance. We understand the word *sin* to stand here for a *sin-offering*. "If thou doest not well—if thou art a sinner—there is a sin-offering by the very door; bring it to my altar." Cain was hindered by his own wilful refusal to obey the plain instructions God had given. He was willing to do something in a religious way; but to humble himself to God's demands, to confess his sins, to rely for forgiveness upon the shedding of blood, he stoutly refused.

Besides expostulating with Cain for his unreasonable rejection of the atonement, the Lord added a mild and forbearing reproof of his temper towards his brother. He concedes the elder brother's privileges; but reminds him that Abel's acceptance was not the cause of his rejection; and thus wonderfully does God deal with men. By the teachings of his word, by the admonitions of their own consciences, and by the strivings of his Holy Spirit, he reminds them that they are the authors of their own destruction; he forbears with them, though they are wayward and unreasonable, he still points out to them his methods of mercy, and waits to be gracious even when they perversely quarrel with him, and with humble worshippers more acceptable than themselves. Yet how mad is sinful man! Despite the offered mercy of God, he will go on to greater and more desperate sin. We are not indeed to suppose that Cain foresaw the end of his course, or thought that the bad passions he now cherished would ere long hurry him into a crime which, as yet upon the earth, was without a name. The methods of sin were then, as now, deceitful. But it was in spite of solemn and tender warnings that Cain passed on to greater sin.

These are important lessons to learn from the history of Cain, before we pass on to the lamentable scenes of his later life:

1. That they who worship God must come in faith; that is, not only acknowledging "that he is, and that he is the rewarder of those that diligently seek him," but recognizing that the diligent seeking of God requires us to lay aside our pride, and to come as he directs us. We are to search after God. The plain way to our darkened reason, may not be, is not likely to be, the right way. Since the world began, no sinner ever found God's favour except through propitiatory services, significant of the shedding of Christ's precious blood. And in these later times, in vain does any man expect

mercy, who neglects the great salvation. Men may differ very much from the temper and conduct of Cain; they may abhor the great crime that has stamped his name with infamy; but if they so far agree with Cain as to neglect atoning blood as he did, God will as certainly reject them as he rejected Adam's first-born son.

2. They whom God reproves by his word, his ministry, his providence, or his Spirit for their wrong methods of worship, have nothing to gain from the indulgence of murmuring or rebellious thoughts. God often refuses to hear our prayers. We cry, but we get no answer. He has always wise reasons for refusal, and even for delay. Let us search and try our ways. Let us watch against anger, pride, and despair. "If thou doest well, thou shalt be accepted;" and in any case let us draw near, pleading the precious name of our sin-offering.

3. Such religious convictions as do not bring the soul near to God, usually tend to harden the heart. Worse than the first, is the last state of a man whose thoughts ponder his duty to God, but who does not truly submit to God's methods of righteousness. The time when a man draws near to God, especially if he has some sense of his need of forgiveness, is a critical time indeed. But God is justified, for the pride, and impenitence, and rebellion of ungodly men, who rebel against his

mercy, and forbearance, and willingness to be gracious.

4. Nothing is more dreadful than quarrelling with God. The wrong is always with us. it leads on to greater evil, and the end is death.

CHAPTER XXIX.

THE SACRIFICE OF ABEL.

BESIDES the remarkable facts already noted concerning sacrifices: that their origin is nowhere expressly recorded; that they are so widely spread among the children of men; and that they explain themselves as significant of propitiation for sin; we may notice other things that possess interesting significance. The animals offered in sacrifice have always been peaceful animals. It was never the lion, the tiger, or the bear; usually the gentle lamb, or the meek heifer. It was also the most useful animals; and to increase the value of offerings which at best seemed too small, a large number of victims were slain. Usually too the distinction was made between clean and unclean animals. In all this seemed significant the truth that peace and holiness must be sought by man of his offended God at any price; and that his gentlest, and purest, and best offerings could but faintly foreshadow the appointed Lamb of the latter days.

If our minds could be carried back to the earliest days of human worship; if we could see our first father Adam by the direct command of God offer upon his rude altar the first sacrificial victim; if we could enter into the feelings of that trembling pair as they stood pleading before their God, we might learn a solemn lesson, not unsuitable to us, even in these days of clearer light. Here have we the same mingling of the awful and the merciful, that may usually be found in the dispensations of God towards man. Adam must be the first Priest. Deeply affected by the unexpected and undeserved mercy of the Lord, he selected the purest and mildest of those mute companions which next to man were the chief ornaments of Paradise. Then he must build an altar; must lead the victim before it; must lay his hands solemnly upon its head, and there confess in the presence of his Maker his wilful, guilty apostasy. This done, the life of the victim must be taken. Awful sight! Blood had never before stained the earth, our first parents had never seen the crimson tide. Now they see the innocent lamb, fainting, gasping, convulsed, and dying. They must see death in this form, and know that their sin had introduced it in worse forms than this.

But it was not all terror that gathered around the bleeding victim and the smoking altar. The main design was to signify and seal the most amazing mercy. It was the first institution of a sacrament in the church of God; and it proclaimed, amid the early ruins of the fall, the same gospel of salvation in which we are called to trust. We have already pointed out the difference between the offerings of Adam's eldest sons; we have seen the true cause of Cain's rejection. It may now be proper for us to consider the principles involved in the sacrifice of Abel. For this is the first offering that is expressly mentioned.

We may suppose that the ceremonies of sacrifice have been substantially the same from the beginning; and that the minute directions of the Book of Leviticus simply record the practices already familiar. When Abel brought of the first and fattest of his flock as an offering to God, he confessed his sin, his helplessness, his righteous exposure to the wrath of God. He laid his hands upon the victim's head; he confessed his sin. Such an offering was unnecessary except for a sinner. The righteous have no need of atonement; the self-righteous feel no need of it. Cain, we have seen, was willing to acknowledge that there was a God; that God was his maker, his providential benefactor; that the fruits of the earth were God's gifts; and that he was dependent upon God as his sovereign. But Cain came not as a sinner with an offering that sought the Divine mercy. He claimed yet to stand as did Adam in Paradise. Abel's offering is significant of Abel's views and feelings. He felt himself a sinner and came as such. And truth and honour were with Abel rather than Cain. Let not the proud and wicked heart of man admire the bold independence of Cain; or take Abel's humility and penitence as tokens of degradation. The reverse is a true judgment. Falsehood is always mean, however proud; and truth is always noble, however humble. To be a sinner is a shameful thing; to be a proud, and stubborn, and hardened sinner is far more shameful. The pride of Cain was wicked in itself, and unbecoming his place; while his brother, if meek, was also truthful. Cain was only the more a sinner, because he refused to confess that he was so. Penitence is the true nobleness of a man, who knows that he is in the wrong, and he commits a greater wrong, who shamelessly refuses to acknowledge the truth. "Wo unto them that call evil good and good evil!" We break down the barriers between right and wrong, either when we admire independent wickedness, or when we despise the honest, candid, and truthful confession of wrong. Cain's refusal to own his guilt made that guilt only the greater, and more incontestably proved him a wicked man; while Abel's offering was the honourable acknowledgment of the truth that he was a sinner. It is more honourable to correct a fault than to persist in repeating it; more honourable to speak the truth, however humbling, than to assume false appearances, however bold; and thus Abel was more honourable than Cain. And a sinful man acts never more truly according to the dictates of true honour, than when he bows before God with the candid and penitent confession of his sins.

But if the sacrifice of Abel was a token of his penitence, it was just as truly a token of his faith. In the Epistle to the Hebrews we are told, "By FAITH Abel offered a more excellent sacrifice than Cain." We do not understand simply that he believed that some benefit would follow the offering. This is true; but to some extent it was true of Cain. Cain expected some advantage to result from his offering; otherwise he would not have brought it at all. Expectation of good, even confidence that we shall receive it, is not the scriptural idea of faith. Faith is the belief of the Divine word, and reliance upon the Divine promise. Cain seems to have trusted not the Divine teachings, but his own reason. And because we cannot see how reason would suggest the offering of Abel, and especially because we are told that he came in faith, we understand that he acted under Divine instruction. If his was a sinner's offering, it was no less the offering of a believer.

Something of the great method of redemption was set forth by it. No thoughtful and serious mind could suppose that such an offering could atone for sin. A deeply convicted conscience would say with Paul, "It is impossible that the blood of bulls and goats could take away sin." Doubtless even in Abel's own eyes, his offering was typical. It began a long line of dark but significant prophecies, where, under the Spirit's teachings, the eye learned much, and the heart far more. It was a pledge, divinely appointed, that the woman's seed should come; it was a pre-intimation of His sufferings, when the Lamb of God should take away sin.

How clear or how obscure were Abel's views, we cannot say. He saw not as we do. He was one of the righteous men, who desired to see the days we see, and saw them not. Perhaps the apostle means this when he says that we are come "to the blood of sprinkling that speaketh better things than that of Abel." Some indeed suppose that he refers to Abel's own blood, which, shed upon the ground, as with the voice of justice, demanded vengeance upon his murderer; and this he contrasts with the blood of Christ, which, as with the merciful voice of the dying sufferer, pleads for forgiveness upon them that slew him. But the apostle may be understood to speak of the blood of Abel's sacrifice. This typified and promised pardon, but did not set this forth as does the blood of Christ that speaketh better things.

The difference between the two brothers was just that of piety and impiety, faith and unbelief in the teachings of Divine truth. It seems shocking to us that the first-born of the human family should so rebel against God, and should refuse the offers of Divine mercy revealed for his salvation. And yet why should so many in later times, and with the clear teachings of the gospel of Christ, repeat the sin of Cain! The same divisions are found in other families besides that of our first parents; and in every case they involve the same eternal interest, the same neglect of Divine mercies. Indeed every soul of those who hear the gospel, is a follower of the guilt of Cain, or of the penitence of Abel.

CHAPTER XXX.

THE DEATH OF ABEL.

THE difference between Cain and Abel was chiefly religious. We may wonder that two brothers could not live peaceably together, though they were thus divided; but we may remember that there is no more important thing than religious faith; nor have any differences between men ever produced more serious results. The sacred writings assure us that the hostility of man's natural mind against piety cannot possibly be reconciled. "The carnal mind is enmity against God, for it is not subject to the law of God, neither indeed can be." The Apostle John expressly declares that Cain hated Abel, "because his own works were evil and his brother's righteous." They had been trained up in the same family; and this under circumstances peculiarly favourable. Christian parents now find it a great hindrance to their family rule, that many families around them are far less careful of their children; and that thus those under their care are exposed to pernicious examples. Nothing of this kind influenced the family of Adam; our first father doubtless taught his children alike the ways of God; and Cain and Abel from such a household should have lived together in unity.

But the differences between them gradually increased; and it was perhaps at the end of many years that the contrast in character became so wide. We must not allow the brevity of the narrative to crowd out of view the real progress of time. It is likely that Abel lived one hundred and twenty-five or one hundred and thirty years. The two brothers were not children in age, knowledge, or experience. From their boyhood they had started in different paths; these did not apparently lead in opposite ways, but they insensibly diverged; and at the end of a century of progress they were far apart. Let two boys start together now from the same family, or the same Sabbath-school. They may seem to differ so little, that parents and friends hope well for both. But when both are forty years old, especially if both live to see sixty or eighty years, each walking in the same path they have early chosen, they will be far apart indeed. If they have loved different things, and held different opinions so long, there is very little likelihood that they will feel or think alike.

When a man has rebelled against God for more than a hundred years, we need not wonder to hear that he hates those whom God loves; nor be surprised at any act of wickedness he may do. We are told that Cain rose up against his brother and slew him. The expression, he talked with him, seems to imply a treacherous concealment of his purpose. Yet it may be that the act was not premeditated; but the result of sudden passion as they talked together. This would make the crime less flagrant; but it was a grievous crime in the mildest view we can take of it. It was the act of one in mature years; the stroke of an elder brother whose place it was rather to protect the younger; the stroke of a wicked man against a righteous man; and here, indeed, as Matthew Henry remarks, Cain struck a blow at God himself, for it was the Divine approbation of Abel that led to this severer hatred.

We have no detailed account of this dreadful scene. It seems to mark it as deliberate, that the fratricide denied all knowledge of his brother, when inquiry was made for him. Perhaps his guilt prompted him to conceal the body; but the deed could not be hid. Reserving to another chapter our thoughts upon the murderer and the dealings of Providence with him, there are two other directions towards which our thoughts may turn, as we reflect upon the death of Abel.

What a stroke of grief was the death of Abel to his parents! Doubtless Adam and Eve had already been deeply grieved with the growing waywardness and wickedness of their eldest born; and the remembrance of their own apostasy was more bitter and humiliating as they saw the proofs of his depravity. But that their anxious watchings for their children should ever bring them to a day like this, was grief and wo, indeed. The day when death first enters the household is a serious one for any family. And when death comes by the stroke of violence, and the form of one we have loved is marred by the murderer's hand, it is inexpressibly more afflicting than the fall of a brother by the touch of Providence. But what horror aggravates the deed when the slayer and his victim have been borne and nursed by the same mother! And here was the first scene of the kind; the first human death was here, and in this bruised and stiffened form Adam saw its terrible reign begin.

We have often been in the house of sorrow. We have seen the aged parent bend over the cold remains of a son cut down in the prime of manhood; and we have dropped the tear of sympathy for those whose stay in declining years has been taken away. But here was affliction in all its novelty; they had no familiarity with death in any form; perhaps no conception of it in a form like this. And yet it was not grief for the dead that filled Adam's family with sorrow in that mournful day. This great grief was swallowed up and forgotten in a greater wo. As for Abel there was hope in his death. The fire of that accepted altar threw its light even across the dark valley now first traversed by man;

and God's acceptance on earth was the earnest of God's acceptance from earth. Abel was not Adam's lost son. In the expressive words we sometimes hear, "*living* trouble IS trouble."

What a flood of wretchedness overwhelms these parents at this first death scene? Had death come in its mildest form, his stroke would have fallen heavily upon them, who had first heard his name in the innocence of Eden, and had themselves given him power in the earth through their folly. But it was not that silent beloved one that gave them grief. It was not the present, dead Abel; it was the absent, conscience-stricken Cain, for whom their parents grieved. We cannot think that Cain would venture to stand by, when they first looked upon the body of Abel. And when the weeping parents must put their dead away out of sight, they could not curse his destroyer; for he too was their son. For Abel they could have dried their tears; for Cain they must flow. Could they have utterly disowned him, his banishment might be some relief. But the wretched and guilty wanderer was still their first-born; and they could not curse him, while also they could not bless. To them might well be spoken the words of Jeremiah, "Weep ye not for the dead, neither bemoan him; but weep sore for him that goeth away." Jer. xxii. 10. No parental grief exceeds their wretchedness who are called to lament for the sin of a beloved child.

But there is another direction in which our

thoughts may turn. Let us think neither of Cain, nor of Adam, but of Abel. That was doubtless a moment of horror when he caught the fierce gleam of his angry brother's eye and saw the threatened blow. Death itself was a new and terrible thing; but for a righteous man to die by a brother's hand, was horror indeed. Unexpected death, death coming suddenly in the very midst of life, is awful enough; but no death can well be more solemn than the first death. "Death was denounced to man as a curse; yet behold it is first inflicted on the innocent."* Sin and death seem indeed to triumph over fallen man.

But the horror of Abel's death is all to sense; our faith may see far different things. Could we lift aside the veil that divides time from eternity, how differently would we feel! As to outward circumstances, Abel did not depart as a believer might desire to. If he saw the descending stroke, his mind could scarcely turn towards the calm reflections and the humble prayers with which the pious soul would wish to meet the last enemy. Composure, meditation, the actual exercise of faith, religious triumph seem all improbable, at an hour like that. It is not needful that the death scene should be rapturous or calm or even peaceful. Anguish and horror may be the last thought. Nor do we read that the first martyr of the Old Testament was like the first martyr of the New. We hear no prayers like those

* Bishop Hall.

of Stephen, "Lord, receive my spirit: lay not this sin to their charge." We read of no opening heavens, and the Son of man waiting to receive the first trophy of recovering grace.

Yet Abel died in faith; and there was an open door in heaven to receive his ascending spirit. Death only *seemed* to triumph over the fallen believer. The first man to die; the first to live for ever; the first mortal for whom the doors of the celestial paradise are opened; the first sinner to sing the song of redeeming love; the first born of glory; surely if these things are true of Abel, he triumphed over death. Happy believer, the first of the long succession of redeemed ones from earth!

What a sad and joyful day was that when Abel died! It was both the triumph and the defeat of death. Sin and death united their forces to compass his murder; but they were able to hold under their power only the corruptible body. Abel himself rose from the red-stained earth to know their power no more for ever. And Satan saw the first evidence of his defeat, as the dying believer triumphed over death and him that has the power of death.

CHAPTER XXXI.

THE CRIMINAL EXPOSED.

We see in Cain the same disposition to conceal his guilt that Adam had before shown. This indeed is characteristic of guilt; and proves the working of conscience. It is true that if the conscience of a guilty man was fully obeyed, it would influence him to confess his iniquity: and yet the shame that hides a crime as truly springs from a sense of guilt. Men do not hide their useful and innocent actions. What we are ashamed of, we should beware of.

As with Adam, so with Cain, God spoke to awaken his conscience. He asked for Abel, his brother. Had there been any penitent thoughts in the heart of Cain after his dreadful deed, this form of inquiry was adapted to call them forth. But, unhappily, Cain was not penitent. His reply therefore was falsehood and insolence. It was bad enough to say, I know not. Had he stopped at this, we might have found this excuse at least of the falsehood, that he feared the discovery of his sin and the results it might bring upon him. Even then it was the folly of guilt, how often since repeated! to think that man's denial can hide the truth from the knowledge of God. But he did not stop with the untruth. He cast away from him the cords with which the Almighty has bound the heart of every man to his brother and his fellow. With an effrontery and insolence, which surely seem to belong to a hardened offender, he asks, Am I my brother's keeper? Am I bound to have any care over him? Are his interests any concern of mine? May he not go where he will, do as he pleases, be what he chooses, and suffer as he may; and all this while I attend to my own affairs, and have nothing to do with him?

There is truly a sense in which every man is the keeper of himself; there are responsibilities which rest upon the individual soul, and which cannot and should not be divided with any other. Each man is responsible for his own character, feelings, thoughts, words, deeds, and omissions as he cannot be for whatever other men may be, or do. But it is no interference with the entireness of individual responsibility that no man does or can live as a separate and independent being. It is a part of an individual responsibility rather, that what we do, and what we refrain from doing, must be governed as truly by the law of God, as what we are and what we feel. There is no dividing line that can run between us and our neighbours, separating our interests from theirs, and defrauding neither when a division is secured. Only in the indulgence of an impious and irreligious spirit can any man fail to recognize the obligations which bind him to every fellow in the race of man.

It is easy to see in the inquiry here made of Cain that that great second principle of the Divine law, "Thou shalt love thy neighbour as thyself," is the recognized foundation of human duty from the beginning. Because Cain was bound thus to love his brother, the question is asked. Because he would throw off the restraints of law, the insolent reply is uttered. And whoever now excuses himself from deeds of charity to the poor, from efforts to spread the gospel in lands of darkness, from schemes of usefulness on every hand, upon the plea that he has no interest in these things, but repeats the falsehood of the first murderer, and affirms that he is not his brother's keeper. It is in no wise possible to multiply the murderous deeds of Cain more abundantly than by filling the minds of men with this sentiment of Cain. When men care little what becomes of their neighbours, it is an easy step to care little what they do to them. The omission indeed of duty may be both as flagrant and as fatal as the actual deed of wickedness. And no man can rightly take care of his own interests and his own soul without the assistance to this end that is afforded by his concern for the interests of others. It is for individual as well as public good, that men should love their neighbours as themselves.

Cain's falsehood was vain. The Divine word so addresses him as to call forth the true temper of his mind; but he soon learns that his sin is not hidden. God declared that he heard the voice of his brother's blood crying from the ground. This, of course, is a figurative expression; but it is exceedingly forcible to declare that sin is never concealed from the Divine Judge, and that its very commission is a call upon him to execute merited punishment. This is true of every sin, the most secret, and the least influential; it is especially true of the greater sins against society and against God, of which Abel's murder was the first fearful example. If, on the one hand, no man can ever commit any sin without the liability that it may one day rise up to meet him, clothed in terrors that shall fill his soul with remorse and horror; so especially, on the other hand, the history of the race is full of the remarkable revelations of crimes, which the providence of God or the conscience of the criminal, perhaps after long years, has brought forth from the mysteries of concealment and denial.

It is not enough that no eye saw the deed of darkness, and that the knowledge of it seems hidden alone in that breast that is too deeply interested ever to make it known. You have doubtless read the strong words of Daniel Webster upon the trial of a criminal, where he urges that the world has no corner dark enough to hide the guilty. "True it is," says he, "that Providence has so ordained and doth so govern things, that those who break the great law of heaven by shedding man's blood, seldom succeed in avoiding discovery. Especially in a case exciting so much attention as this, discovery must come, and will come, sooner or later. A thousand eyes turn at once to explore every man, every thing, every circumstance connected with the time and place; a thousand ears catch every whisper, a thousand excited minds intensely dwell on the scene, shedding all their light and ready to kindle, at the slightest circumstance, into a blaze of discovery.

"Mean time, the guilty soul can not keep its own secret. It is false to itself, or rather it feels an irresistible impulse to be true to itself. It labours under its guilty possession, and knows not what to do with it. The human heart was not made for the residence of such an inhabitant . . . The secret which the murderer possesses, soon comes to possess him; and like the evil spirits of which we read, it overcomes him and leads him whithersoever it will . . . He thinks the whole world sees it in his face, reads it in his eyes, and almost hears its workings in the very silence of his thoughts. It has become his master. It betrays his discretion, it breaks down his courage, it conquers his prudence. When suspicions from without begin to embarrass him, and the net of circumstances to entangle him, the fatal secret struggles with still greater violence to burst forth."

There is upon this subject an unjust and unwise prejudice against admitting that circumstantial evidence can prove beyond a question the commission of a crime. Yet if circumstantial evidence may not be received to convict a man of crime, the most flagrant offences must pass unpunished. For the more deliberate a murder is, the more likely it is to be committed when no witnesses are present. When a man strikes at the life of his neighbour in sudden anger, he may do the deed in open day, and with no regard to the numerous witnesses that may surround him. But no man will form the deliberate purpose of crime, and then prefer to do the deed where it can certainly be proved upon him. As men are prone to deny their guilt when it is charged upon them, so they take every possible care to prevent any proof that may lead to their conviction. "He that doeth evil hateth the light;" and no human witnesses see the crimes that most deserve to be punished.

Not only will the most flagrant crimes remain unpunished, if we always require direct witnesses of their commission; but the real proof of the deed may be even less certain. It is a great mistake to judge that circumstantial evidence is more fallacious than direct proof. Since perjury is possible, the explicit testimony of a few witnesses may really be of far less weight than a well established train of circumstances. When public attention is fully aroused by some shocking crime, when everybody's ears and lips are open, and from a hundred witnesses, who do not know each other, or know what each other says, an array of minute facts is gathered, each of small account in itself, and yet all together forming a train of connected circumstances—like the types of a printed page, each type of little significance, yet this combination of them all, conveying most important instruction—there is often secured a conclusive proof scarcely inferior to the sight of the eyes. In a well established chain of such evidences, the witnesses cannot possibly agree to make any false impression. They are too numerous and of too diverse characters; many of them cannot know the bearing upon the case of the little thing they have to say; it is impossible to make a long array of falsehoods hang harmoniously together; and though it is possible for many suspicious circumstances to array themselves around an innocent man, it is also true that clearly defined circumstantial proof may gather a network of evidence around a criminal to hem him in on every side; and we may decide upon his guilt with as much certainty as ever belongs to human judgments. On such proof a conclusion may be founded, "far more satisfactory than direct evidence can produce." *

* Greenleaf on Evidence, i. 19.

CHAPTER XXXII.

CAPITAL PUNISHMENT.

It seems fairly implied in the language used concerning Cain that the natural and proper punishment for the crime of murder is the death of the criminal. The cry of the blood from the ground, and the apprehension of Cain that whosoever found him would kill him, seem to teach this, before we have any expressed law upon the subject. Nor does the fact that Cain was not put to death, furnish any argument against the righteousness of the principle. Rather, the manner of his exemption is a proof of the law. For evidently Cain felt that he deserved to die; he knew that others felt so too; and nothing less than some kind of a mark from God himself was able to protect him from the strong sense of retributive justice in the minds of men that he ought to die. Unless we deny that even God can grant exemption, we should admit that such a mark upon the murderer to keep men from doing what otherwise they would do, is the strongest proof that this sentiment was originally and deeply implanted in the human mind.

In the times in which we live many efforts have been made to show that capital punishment ought not to be inflicted. Among the errors by which this opinion is urged upon the attention of society these are prominent:

1st. It is urged that the proper end of punishment is the reformation of the offender and the prevention of further crimes, and that therefore the death penalty can never be justly inflicted. It may be acknowledged that the civil law ought to deal tenderly, especially with offenders whose consciences are not utterly hardened; that every proper means should be used to reclaim them; and that to restrain men from doing like things is an important end in administering justice. But it is a radical mistake to allege that the true nature of punishment is to be sought in either of these things. We call this the administration of justice. But justice means just this—that the criminal receives *what he deserves.* Some crimes are worse than others, in their own nature, and in their aggravating circumstances, and in their results. Hence punishments differ. But all punishments should or should not be inflicted, according to the desert of the individual. If the worst man in the land was apprehended and punished for some crime of which he was innocent, no plea of benefit to be conferred upon him, could free such a sentence from the charge of injustice. Guilt is the only thing that can justify any kind of punishment; men are therefore punished because they deserve it. And no other valuable influence can ever spring from the administration of law, unless this lies at the foundation of all, that justice is done. Men are punished not for expediency's sake, nor for the sake of reformation; but because they deserve it.

2d. It is urged that capital punishments come to us from the old Mosaic laws, and the abrogation of these takes away all the force of authority which would establish such a kind of punishment among us. We may freely admit that many of the precepts given through Moses to the Jewish people are not binding upon us; and that we are in no wise bound to copy either the laws or the punishments that were directly adapted to the Jewish people. It is not because such laws were given to them, that we argue the propriety of the death penalty for the crime of murder. That the Jewish people, or any people, ever had the right, by Divine authority, to take away life, does indeed prove that the power of civil government over the lives of its citizens does not at all depend upon their consent granted to that effect; and that having once been just it cannot now be *essentially* and *radically* unjust.

But we affirm that the penalty of death for the crime of murder dates further back than the origin of the Jewish people; that it does not belong to their commonwealth, and is not a peculiarity of the Theocratic government; and that therefore neither its propriety nor authority is affected by the passing away of the Jewish dispensation. In this record concerning Cain, we have the propriety of this punishment recognized at the very origin of human society; and when after the deluge society was reconstructed for all mankind in our second father, Noah, no language can be more explicit than the charge given to all men and all time through him. Where is the evidence that God ever repealed these words? They were not spoken to the Jews, but to man. "Whoso sheddeth man's blood by man shall his blood be shed." And if there was any force in the reason assigned, it is as forcible in one land or age, as another; "For in the image of God made he man."

If it can be proved that the practice of putting men to death for the crime of murder prevailed only among the Jewish people, there might be more force in the allegation that such a penalty should cease with the fall of the Jewish State. But the universal prevalence of the sentiment forbids us to think that it either belonged specially to Jewish law, or was copied by men from the Jewish statute book. That the penalty of death has been inflicted in every land, and under every style of government, declares it the natural dictate of man's sense of justice.

3d. It is urged against capital punishment sometimes that it is too severe, and at other times that it is not sufficiently severe. These contradictory statements sometimes occur in the same argument;

and prove but little for the candor of those who urge them.

It is vain for any man to argue that death is a punishment less severe than a lifelong imprisonment. Men do not plead for death rather than imprisonment: criminals never ask their attorneys to secure for them, if possible, the conviction of murder in the first degree, rather than the second, because the first has the milder punishment of death; or if a man was sentenced to a life imprisonment for some great offence, men would not consider it an act of mercy, should a mob wrest him from the hands of the officers and hang him on the road to the penitentiary. Whatever instances of morbid folly may be adduced to the contrary, it is the common and just sentiment of mankind, that death is the severest penalty that human law can inflict.

And just because it is so, it ought to be inflicted for the highest crime of which man can be guilty. There are men who, without having shed blood, are so injurious to society that they deserve a lifelong separation from their fellows. But so precious a thing is human life; so widely should we separate between the crime that takes this away and every other crime, that the highest possible penalty is not too severe for its punishment. Nor is there the slightest force in the cavil that we thus repeat the very offence which we punish. There is the greatest possible difference between the same things done by violence and done by law; done by private revenge or private vice, and done by public justice. If a magistrate lawfully inflicts a fine upon me, and the sheriff clothed with the proper authority forcibly takes my property to pay that fine; this is one thing. If a robber forcibly takes from me the same amount, it is quite another thing. If the law takes a man's life, it is penalty: if an unauthorized person takes away life, it is murder. Provocation to murder may extenuate the offence; hence the law allows of several degrees; but voluntarily, unlawful killing is always criminal; and by this, is as far as possible removed from the authorized acts of the law. What folly to suppose that the Lawgiver did not understand his own law, when he declared that the blood of the murderer should be shed; or when he followed the general declaration, Thou shalt not kill, by numerous explicit directions to punish certain crimes with death!

Among the reasons that urge that the murderer should certainly be put to death, may be mentioned such as these:

1st. The sacredness of human life and the propriety of throwing every possible safeguard around the innocent. Death is the most solemn event that meets man upon the earth. No greater injury can be inflicted upon any man than to take his life. The man who will wantonly or wickedly commit this highest of all crimes, justly merits the highest of all penalties; this enormous crime should have a punishment of extreme severity.

2d. The direct authority of the Divine law vindicates the righteousness of this penalty. That cannot be in its own nature unrighteous that has so repeatedly received the Divine sanction; and if in some states of society, less crimes than this have been thus punished, this does not weaken the proof that a crime, which all ages and all nations have consented so to punish, should ever require the death of the offender. And no sophistry can evade the direct force of the precept given to Noah, "Whoso sheddeth man's blood by man shall his blood be shed."

3d. If capital punishment is abolished for the crime of murder, human life will be rendered more insecure. Many a wicked man, in the eager pursuit, for slight or even fancied injuries, will run almost any risk to wreak the severest revenge. Let such a man know that his own life is safe in any event, even when he takes the life of his neighbour, and he will not stay his hand from this foulest deed. So if there is no greater punishment for murder, than for robbery, many a witness will be put out of the way; with the hope that both crimes may escape detection, and with the certainty that the discovery of the two can make the sentence little or nothing more severe. To lay aside the death penalty from our statute book is to throw the influence of our laws around the criminal for his protection, while we leave just men more exposed to violence than over. Let us sympathize with suffering, but not to legalize violence; not to allow criminals to do what none but they dare do. A French writer upon this subject forcibly sums it all up in a single expression. "If the flow of human blood should stop, let the murderers set the example!" Just as soon as men cease to take away the lives of their fellows by wrong, capital punishment by law may cease; and the last can never safely be laid aside till the first is no longer known.

4th. So strong is the sense of indignation and right in human minds against foul crimes, that to abolish capital punishments will certainly tend to increase the cases in which human life will be sacrificed. How comes it to pass that in our own land, among the most intelligent and law-abiding people upon earth, we have so many instances of Lynch Law and of Vigilance Committees? If the laws will not do what the moral sense of the community declares should be done, means will be found to reach the end. Yet far better execute justice by law, than by the power of the most respectable Committee of Vigilance that ever existed.

Nor, 5th, does human experience show that the penalty of death can be justly or wisely laid aside. The trial has been made, and not without serious remonstrance against its influence. We need not attempt to gather here statistics upon such a subject; but may simply express the hope that the public convictions are more settled in support of the death penalty than the agitations of the subject seemed to threaten a few years ago.

The Divine law upon the subject is the earliest instance of legislation; it was repeated the first of laws when the world was repeopled; it is comprehensive in its terms; it has the same reasons to enforce it now as ever. God gave it; he has never repealed it. And his law and the sense of justice in every human breast are violated by its repeal. No reasons exist why man can ever wisely or justly set himself in array against the Divine Legislator.

CHAPTER XXXIII.

THE PUNISHMENT OF CAIN.

THE question may naturally be asked, Why was the penalty of death remitted to the first murderer? If human life is so sacred, and should be so sacredly guarded, why should the example be so early set of the exemption of a manslayer whose guilt was so aggravated, and whose evil influence might be so wide and great?

The remission of a penalty is no disproof of its justice. If we cannot give any good reason for the fact that God not only exempted, but also protected the first murderer from the vengeance of man, this does not invalidate the proof that the law was ordinarily otherwise. The necessity of a mark upon Cain arose from the law; and if God should now put a well known mark upon any man, signifying the Divine will that we should not punish him, we ought to regard this as a proper reason for remitting the penalty. But surely the reasoning would be too absurd to say: since God remitted this penalty, every penalty should be remitted, and no murderer punished! The power of remitting or commuting punishment ever belongs to sovereign authority; its exercise must be governed by the discretion of the executive; and the law is still the same, even when we cannot explain why this clemency is shown.

We do not know for what reason God remitted the penalty of death for the sin of Cain. But it is not hard to see that one reason would make his punishment more difficult and delicate than that of any subsequent manslayer, and would render the remission of his punishment almost as much a favour to others as to himself. If Cain should have been put to death not long after his offence, we may ask the question, By whose hands must the sentence be executed? Cain was himself the oldest man on the earth, except his own father; and as Adam had no childhood, but was created a mature man, perhaps his eldest son, though he would appear much younger, was really only a year or two younger than his father. By whose hands then must Cain die, if the law was carried out? Must Adam take the life of his first born? If not he, then the circle of men next younger were Cain's own brothers. Must they execute the law against him? It seemed necessary in the circumstances of the case to choose between these two things: either to delay the death of Cain until a generation of men had grown up who were but distantly related; or to lay the heavy burden of putting him to death upon some near and tender relative. This was the unparalleled state of things that this unhappy criminal was a near relative of every living soul upon the earth; and though justice did require his death, yet it could not then occur without doing violence to the tenderest feelings of humanity. God's leniency towards the murderer was to spare the feelings of others. The law could be carried out without such a sacrifice of feeling in later times. It could not then. Nor is this the only instance in which the circumstances of Adam's family tended to modify the laws afterwards enforced.

But if the living men were all his near kindred, why did Cain fear that some man finding him would kill him? Doubtless there were men enough living on the earth at that time; for the increase of Adam's family may have been rapid. But no matter how numerous they are, they were all near relatives. But there is no necessity for supposing that Cain's fears all referred to the present time. Perhaps Cain lived more than six hundred years after the death of Abel; by that time the earth would be covered with a large population; some of these would be far removed from him in relationship; and without the assurance of Divine protection, he might be liable to be put to death at any time. It is God's design that since Cain does not die in immediate connection with his crime, he shall not live for ages in apprehension that the stroke may one day come.

But though that, which we regard as the natural penalty of Cain's crime, was for this or other reasons remitted, he was not wholly without punishment. The mere discovery of crime has often the effect to awaken remorse in the criminal, which he has not felt so long as his crime remained unknown. Especially the voice of God can easily arouse the slumbering conscience of the guilty. Even after such a crime, Cain uttered a lie in his Maker's presence, and with bold-browed insolence refuses to be interrogated as his brother's keeper. But soon the scene changes; his heart is filled with terror; and he hears with dismay the sentence that hardens the earth beneath him; and sends him forth a restless, unhappy wanderer from the tents of his father and the presence of God. Away from God's sight he could not go; perhaps there was some manifestation of God in a place of appointed worship; perhaps any worship that Cain might offer could no longer have hope of acceptance.

The conscience of a sinner may be long careless; new engagements in life, new crimes against God or man may harden the heart; but at any moment the transgressor is liable to an awakening by the voice of God or the finger of Providence, that shall banish all his false peace. Happy is he whose conscience is early awakened. Happy he who truly repents of sin, and implores the Divine mercy when God speaks to his conscience! We know not how to interpret the complaint of Cain; but it is evidently the voice of misery, however we understand it. If we take the words just as they stand in the

English Bible, "My punishment is greater than I can bear:" we may know that a man may have in his own breast a sense of wretchedness through his own sins, the most insupportable. There are some who argue that the punishments of sin are through the conscience alone; and that every transgressor even in this life receives constantly the just reward of his transgressions. This is teaching very different from human experience, and from the word of God. Human experience teaches that the more men sin, the more indifferent ordinarily do they become to the commission of sin; and the Bible teaches that "because sentence against an evil work is not executed speedily, therefore the hearts of the children of men are fully set within them to do evil." To say that men always feel the remorse due to their sins in this life, is to express an error dangerous in its tendencies and unsupported by any wise teachings. To affirm that they are *sometimes* awakened to keen remorse, and that then their anguish is grievous to be borne, is a truth of immense importance. For if, even here, God lays his heavy hand upon the transgressor, when there are so many things around to alleviate his sorrows and to engage his thoughts, who can bear the anguish of that world of woe, where all reasons for Divine forbearance will be gone, and the soul shall only bear his wrath?

It implies the anguish of Cain's mind, if we take his words in another sense, which may belong to them, and which is expressed in the marginal reading of the English Bible: "Mine iniquity is greater than that it may be forgiven." We do not know that Cain had sinned beyond the Divine forgiveness. Rather, the true scheme of Divine mercy from one end to the other of this sacred volume, encourages even great transgressors to return to God and live. But this wretched man before this refused to draw near to God in the appointed methods of his worship; and now, in the time of his acknowledged guilt, he shows no disposition to adopt that system of faith, on account of which he had slain his brother. We have no reason to doubt that God's forbearance towards him gave him opportunities for repentance. But we have no evidence that he ever did repent. The reverse seems to be taught us. Cain went out from the presence of the Lord. Away from the place of God's appointed worship; away from the society of those that loved and feared God, he voluntarily went forth. This is the crowning proof of Cain's impenitence; this marks the essential distinction between remorse and repentance. There is a sorrow for sin that is a sorrow of the world; its mark is, that it drives a man away from God and piety, and its end is death. There is a godly sorrow, that grieves before God, and leads the penitent towards God, seeking forgiveness and practising obediences; and this sorrow alone is unto life, and is itself not to be repented of.

Sin is a fearful thing; but impenitence in view of God's forbearance and mercy, greatly aggravates iniquity, and more clearly justifies God's condemnation of the sinner. Great a sinner as Cain was, his sin was greater far, for his hardening his spirit in such obstinate unbelief. Doubtless Cain thought hard of God. Impenitence always prompts this feeling. A wise sinner will beware of it. God is holy, wise, and just; we are through sin prone to self-deceit and self-indulgence. That only is true penitence, which both acknowledges the equity of the Divine sentence, and seeks forgiveness through mercy.

Men who may not reach the deep measure of Cain's iniquity, nor go through the earth with the mark of Cain upon them, must still beware that they copy not his impenitence. Let a man's sins be great or small, if he goes out from the presence of the Lord; if he turns away from his gospel, his mercy-seat, and his service, he goes in the way of Cain, and he shall meet the woe of Cain. And every step in this way is dangerous. Wisdom bids the sinful soul stop now; and God's voice pleads, "To-day . . . harden not your hearts."

CHAPTER XXXIV.

CALLING UPON THE LORD.

It is the kind ordination of Divine Providence that time alleviates our most poignant sorrows. The human mind could not long endure the pressure of such griefs as sometimes fall upon us; and though there are sufferings we cannot learn to forget, yet the anguish of such is softened by the demands which new duties make upon our thoughts and cares. Such trouble as had now fallen upon Adam's family, must have cast its gloomy shadow far forward upon the long pathway of their lives. Many an hour of tears, many a pang of bitter grief, would memory bring upon Adam and Eve, as they recalled the death of Abel, and the stern brow and the haughty impenitence of their exiled first born. Yet their minds were engaged and relieved by the healthful occupations of life; and the cares of an increasing household prevented them from brooding over their great grief. Shortly after the murder of Abel another son was born. Him they named Seth; and he was received by Eve as Abel's successor. Yet we believe that many sons and daughters had before this been born to our first parents. We may trust that Seth specially possessed the faith and character of Abel. His descendants received the promises; and through him four thousand years later, the promised Seed was born. On this account the name of Seth is thus specially mentioned of Adam's sons.

After this we have but few words concerning Adam. But the record of the age to which he lived, teaches us that Adam saw eight lineal generations of his children, and died one hundred and twenty-six years before the birth of Noah. The most remarkable occurrences of the antediluvian period occurred while the first father yet lived. He lived to see a vast increase of the world's population, the spread of corruption and violence, and the world fast ripening for the judgments of God. Polygamy sprung up, a fruitful source of evils in all the history of man; and murder became no uncommon event.

But while many dark shades rested upon the picture of human life spread before the eyes of Adam, there were also scenes of joy and cheerfulness. Perhaps one of these is signified by the record made shortly after the birth of Seth, "Then began men to call upon the name of the Lord." Standing by itself, we cannot indeed decide certainly upon the meaning of the expression. Some have even thought that this is a record of evil; and that then first men began to use the name of God profanely. There can be no question but that the proper use of the Divine name would naturally precede the profane use of it; and this is proof of the exceeding wickedness of profane swearing, that it is WORSHIP IN MOCKERY. Profane swearers do not think as they say; nor mean the full wickedness of their words; nor of deliberate purpose insult God, and call for his vengeance. But scarcely any wickedness has less of justifying apologies, is more purely wicked in itself, has a greater direct tendency to dishonour God and bring contempt upon him, and is of less advantage to the transgressor, than the vice of profanity. It is always a social vice. Nobody ever learned to swear by himself, or cared to indulge in profanity, unless after the bad habit was firmly fixed, except in the hearing of others. Thus the profane man is always a sower of mischief. He calls upon all who hear his profane words, and bids them mock God. How any man of common sense and having a single serious thought, not to speak of pious feeling, can read over such a tract as the "Swearer's Prayer," and then ever venture to open his lips in profanity, is most amazing. Yet that men can so do, is proof that the darkest teachings of the Bible concerning human depravity are but too true. What a world of iniquity this is by reason of profanity! The oaths of men far outnumber their prayers; and it is well that God is of long suffering mercy. And many persons, who do not take the name of God in vain, yet venture upon the borders of profanity by many expletives that partake of the same nature, that are useless in themselves, and that are of evil tendency.

But although this form of human wickedness may have prevailed early in the history of the race, we do not think that its origin is here recorded. Nor do the words mean that then men first began to pray. It is indeed striking that the Bible can hardly be said to command us to pray. Its injunctions to this duty seem rather to be directions concerning the manner, the spirit, and the objects of prayer; and thus they take this duty for granted as one of natural obligation, or as a privilege that needs no law to command it. Dr. Dwight remarks that the first command to pray is found in Ps. cxxii. 6. "Pray for the peace of Jerusalem;" and this was given after the world was three thousand years old.* But even this rather exhorts to plead for a special thing, than commands the mere duty of prayer. So our Lord says, "Thou, *when thou prayest*, enter into thy closet." Thus he directs us how to pray, rather than commands the duty. We may believe that to the spiritual mind prayer is as natural as breath to the body. Men could not live one day in a world of wants like this, surely neither Adam nor Abel could be believers in the promises of a merciful God, without prayer. The first promise in Eden was the first encouragement to pray. When Abel stood by his accepted altar, the sacrifice

* Sermon, 141.

itself was a mute prayer; and his faith doubtless gave audible utterance to the emotions of his heart. The Apostle Paul may be understood to teach clearly that prayer is implied in every act of worship. "He that cometh unto God must believe that he is, and that he is the rewarder of them that diligently seek him." Heb. xi. 6. Prayer was scarcely first offered in the days of Enos.

Others suppose that calling upon the name of the Lord, which had its origin in the days of this son of Seth, may signify the first establishment of public worship among men. But we know that the Sabbath was in existence from the beginning; the offering of sacrifices was a public service; and we cannot think that gatherings for worship, which included even small numbers when the inhabitants of the world were few, should be denied the name of public worship. Others refer the meaning of the words to the greater difference which about this time began to prevail between the church and the world. So the marginal reading is, "Then began men to call themselves by the name of the Lord." So a little later we read of intermarriages between the sons of God and the daughters of men. Adam trained his entire family in the same religious faith. The force of education would lead them all to have some respect to piety for a while, even when they were not pious; but gradually throwing off those wholesome restraints, the time came for the clear distinction to mark those who did and those who did not serve God.

But in his "History of Redemption," President Edwards interprets these words in still a different sense. He understands it as the record of the first general and powerful revival of religion among the sons of men. Amidst the corruption that began to overspread the world, Adam had the delight to see a time of the flourishing of true piety. The enemy came in like a flood, and the Spirit of the Lord lifted up a standard against him. As that eminent man remarks, ever since the establishment of the church, God has been pleased to carry forward his work among men by granting times of the remarkable outpouring of his Spirit. There are indeed ordinary workings of the Spirit of God, accompanying the gospel, and making it effectual to the salvation of sinful men, in all ages and lands where his truth is preached. Yet by special seasons of mercy—called, commonly, revivals of religion—he has ever been pleased to glorify his name, and to gather men in greater numbers to partake of his grace. In the days of Enos such a time of refreshing came from the presence of the Lord; and men began to call upon him.

A time of revival calls forth the deep anxiety of God's people. For if then many forsake the world for the service of God, many too remain hardened in sin; many are only almost persuaded to forsake sin; and many indulge transient purposes of penitence and transient joys in a profession of piety. In times of revival the religious feelings of men rapidly tend to an issue; and men soon decide the momentous issues of life or death eternal. A few brief passing days or hours often determine the choice of many immortal souls. Alas! the fatal difference between the sons of Adam still exists, and has grown no less as the world has grown older. Every man still needs the grace of God for his forgiveness and renewal and everlasting life.

As religion and irreligion struggled with each other in the earth, no man could feel a deeper interest in the issue than the father of the race. These were all his children. More than this: When he saw so many depart from God, and fill the earth with violence, he could not forget that by his guilty folly, sin had entered the world. How little repentance can avail to repair the evils man has done, we may learn from the experience of Adam. And his was great joy when he saw some walking in paths of piety. But in every age of the world, and not less among the long-lived men for whose wickedness the flood soon came, few have walked in the way of life; and the broad and downward road has been crowded. As Adam looked upon his increasing race, the words of the curse in Eden were fulfilled, "In sorrow shalt thou eat bread all the days of thy life."

CHAPTER XXXV.

LONG LIFE.

"It is not growing like a tree
In bulk, doth make man better be,
Or standing long an oak, three hundred year
To fall a log at last, dry, bald, and sear;
A lily of a day
Is fairer far in May,
Although it fall and die that night,
It was the plant and flower of light;
In small proportions we just beauties see
And in short measures life may perfect be."

B. JONSON.

THE long lives of men in the early history of the orld are a matter of interest to us, whose term of earthly existence is but one tenth as long. Adam himself may be said to have had as long a period of adult life as any of his children. It may be that some lived a thousand years. The longest life recorded is that of Methuselah: this was 969; ending with the very year of the flood. No decided record is given of the character of Methuselah. As he was in the line of piety and the ancestor of Noah, we may hope that he was a good man; and perhaps the very deluge was delayed until after his removal. If not, perhaps as a wicked man, he perished in this great judgment of God.

The long lives of men made it a more easy thing to transmit the chief events of history from one generation to another. Not more than six or seven persons would be necessary to transmit the earliest portions of the world's history down to the times of Moses. Methuselah lived more than two hundred years contemporaneously with Adam, and one hundred years with Shem; and Adam, Methuselah, and Shem could convey intelligence learned from before the flood, even as far down as the days of Jacob. Thus the witnesses would be few, and the line direct to pass down human traditions; a matter of great importance when men had no written records. Yet we do not depend upon their memories for the accuracy of the history we possess. Even if Moses, our historian of these early times, derived his information originally from oral tradition, the influence of God's Holy Spirit cast out from his records every form of error, and supplied every needful truth. For the holy men of old, in writing the sacred volume, "spake as they were moved by the Holy Ghost."

The length of human life was gradually and rapidly shortened after the flood; so that in the times of Moses men lived to the same term of life now common on the earth. The gradual shortening of the term of existence may be seen by comparing the v.

and the xi. chapters of Genesis. Almost every age in the v. chapter is over nine hundred years; in chapter xi. Shem lived over six hundred years; his three next descendants average less than four hundred and fifty; and the three next two hundred and thirty-five; and the three next less than two hundred. Moses himself lived to the age of one hundred and twenty years; but in Ps. xc. written by him, the usual term of human life is mentioned as seventy years. Even now unusual cases of longevity occur, running up over 160 years. Sixty years ago a man died in Norway aged 160; thirty years ago one died in Russia aged 165. Men may live 90, 100, 120 years, or even more; yet after seventy, their strength is usually "labour and sorrow."

Perhaps the chief reason for the shortening of human life is a moral reason. Our time upon the earth is very brief and unsatisfactory, if this is the only life man is ever to possess. But if the present life is designed to be but preparatory to another and an endless one; if God designs that we should fix our thoughts upon higher service and higher enjoyments than can belong to us here, then the present life is sufficiently long to enable us to prepare for another. This is the season of our minority, and our chief concern should be to use well the important hours, with our eyes fixed upon the more desirable state for which they prepare us. How rare a thing it is to see a child long to remain a child! Rather how children wish the slow years would hasten away that they may be men!

Is it likely that we would prepare better to leave the earth, if the allotted time of our remaining here was lengthened ten fold? Is it not true now that religious thoughts and purposes are delayed in our earlier years, with the hope and promise of future care and repentance? We can scarcely doubt that a long life upon earth—that the hope of living for centuries would operate unfavourably to the religious characters of men. We are not surprised—even judging from the experience we have of human nature—that generations of long-lived men were generations of giants in wickedness, and that the earth was filled with violence. Give men the prospect of living long, and they will usually expect to repent late; and alas! all experience proves that the promise to repent late is usually followed by repenting never. If men pass their early years in folly and sin, there is but little hope that they will begin to fear and serve God when riper years come. Their habits are so strong; their companions possess so much influence; perhaps their past deeds of evil are too shameful to be confessed; perhaps their present engagements are too profitable to be given up; perhaps they have formed prejudices too powerful against religious men and religious teachers. Wonderful and numerous are the ties which bind evil men to evil ways, when they have for years chosen the paths of error. A labyrinth of mazy wanderings is that home of earthly and sinful pleasures in which the Prince of this world receives and entertains his subjects. Few that go with him return; they become more and more entangled; his house is the way to hell, going down to the chambers of death.

If we found by common observation that men after a while became tired of sinning, and turned of their own accord to better courses, we might believe that a long life here would prove favourable to religion and morality. But this is the reverse of human experience. The heart becomes hardened against good and careless of transgression by long habits. How rare and strange the prodigy of the conversion from any evil, say of a man who has been a transgressor for sixty or seventy years! Go into any of the abodes of sin in this land; and use your efforts to reform the guilty. Lift up that fallen form, which intemperance has degraded. Comb back the gray hairs and look upon that marred face. Speak plainly and kindly to that aged heart. How much hope have you that the drunkard of seventy will leave his cups? Can the Ethiopian change his skin or the leopard his spots? And if you cannot dissolve habits that have been strengthened by indulgence for seventy years, what would you do for a wicked man who had lived seven or eight hundred? It is not only habits of intemperance that are by years more inveterate. The very term expresses the usual opinions of men—*in-*

veterate, fixed by age. Every vice is stronger when it is older; and when even the physical energies are too weak to pursue the object, the mind remains the same. We know the power of Divine grace is irresistible; but the change of an aged sinner is a remarkable and uncommon event.

As every sinner hardened in vice becomes a tempter of others; and uses his cunning and influence to seduce others to evil, we need not wonder that wickedness greatly increased in the antediluvian world. When we consider how much more easily evil can be wrought than good, we may well fear to think how much mischief one single bad man could do in a community where he would use efforts to corrupt the youth for fifty years. If the history of some living men could be faithfully written for only ten years back; if we could see how they themselves have grown, in that time, more hardened, more cunning, more heaven-daring; if we could note their numerous secret efforts to corrupt society and to ruin souls; if we could trace the spread of their influence through various victims all over the land, and in coming years, we might well stand appalled at the gathering wickedness of one man in ten years of time. How rich some men will be when their gathered treasures are laid before them at the final day! Rich in the awful wrath of God!

But give that bad man the hope of exemption from the stroke of death for nine hundred years of earthly life; let him have the experience and the cunning and the recklessness which time brings, not for decades but for centuries; and not only may you give up hope of his repentance, but you may confess that one such man in any city, sets at defiance every salutary effort, and puts in peril the best interests of every family that dwells near him. We do not think that longer life than men now ordinarily possess would be favourable to the interests of public morals or a benefit to themselves. If men are disposed to serve God and do good, they live here long enough to show this. The man who can live on earth for forty years careless of God and neglectful of his soul's salvation, may indeed think on his ways and repent and seek the Divine forgiveness afterwards. But so long a period spent in sin and voluntary neglect of God leaves him no room to complain, if a life thus spent should be cut short without experience of the Divine mercy; and it is too true that the likelihood of repentance in such a man rapidly decreases with increasing years. He who will not serve God in a life that may reach to seventy or ninety, would not likely serve him any better in a life of seven or nine hundred. Time enough is now allotted for those that walk here in the ways of piety, to show their love and their zeal for God; and with less experience of sorrow and temptation they are earlier rewarded with the rest and bliss of heaven. Time enough for the working of evil is allotted to those who cast off the obligations of the Divine law; the earth is earlier free from the evil of their example; and they sooner pass to their merited doom. The life of men on earth is short, but long enough if rightly used, and if properly regarded as only the threshold of an eternal existence.

The sacred writers say but little of the dying scenes of any believer's life. We are not told how Adam died. But, nine hundred and thirty years after he had first awaked to life amid the sweet melodies of Paradise, our first father met the curse pronounced upon his early guilt, and returned to his original dust. The brief record of so long a life may suggest to us many profitable reflections. If his long life seemed but a brief and troubled dream, how vain is ours! If this is the record for such a man, how insignificant are we upon the earth! And if our earthly time is given us to prepare for eternity and is long enough—not more—for this purpose, how diligently and with our might we should do what our hands find to do!

And what even is the life of the early patriarchs compared with the endless duration to which we all are hastening forward? What can earth profit the man who fails to lay hold upon an eternal crown?

www.ingramcontent.com/pod-product-compliance
Lightning Source LLC
LaVergne TN
LVHW010218110826
845151LV00004B/1128